HOME

RECIPES FROM IRELAND

The Healy Pass, Beara Peninsula, between Co. Cork and Co. Kerry.

Trish Deseine

HOME

RECIPES FROM IRELAND

Photography : Deirdre Rooney
Styling : Trish Deseine

For Victoire

hachette
CUISINE

Breads from Scarpello & Co. bakery, Ramelton, Co. Donegal.

CONTENTS

Salad leaves from Steven Gould for Kai restaurant, Galway.

A COUNTY ANTRIM CHILDHOOD

"Where's Manuel, Daddy?" the ten-year-old me asked my father at our family tea table. "You're eating him." he said, looking first at the meat on my plate, then at me, half-smiling at the rather brutal comedy, while my two brothers fell about laughing, and my mother rolled her eyes.

When my father was still farming his suckler herd of Herefords, Angus and Shorthorn crosses on County Antrim's (then) rich grasslands, it was my job to feed our farm's orphaned calves in the morning before school — not that I considered this in any way as a chore. Every calving season there was usually a baby whose mother had died after giving birth and I was secretly delighted that their loss meant a new pet for me. With my black Wellington boots over my thick school socks, I would go through the hay sheds to the calves' pen in the dark (I would have to pick off the pieces of hay later on the school bus) and make up pails of powdered milk, trying hard not to splash it on the rest of my uniform as the little calves slurped and stamped, heads bowed unnaturally, but still impatient to get their ration down.

I loved the sweet, vanilla smell of the powder and its cool, velvety feel in my hands. I had learned, by watching my father, how to draw the colostrum from a cow's teat and get the calf hooked on for the first time, its improbably long, pink tongue fixing it right up to the crease of the udder, with hot milk bubbles foaming at the side of its mouth. I learned also how to make motherless calves suck on my fingers instead, before pulling their little muzzles into the buckets of false milk — snorting at first as it went up their noses — to drink.

Cattle, gentle as most of them may be, do not make the most responsive pets. Sometimes, when I was out wandering through our farm's fields, one of the now grown-up calves I had reared would recognize me, break rank and amble over to let its head be scratched again. But that was as far as they, and I, would go. Manuel was named, randomly, after the waiter in *Fawlty Towers*. But despite the daft name, and my fostering duties, I did not become too attached to him, as with all the calves who eventually joined the rest of the herd to grow the meat that made our living. I knew what Manuel's fate would be, even if it was a surprise that evening at the table to hear he had done so well on my pails of powdered milk, and then on our grass, that my father had chosen him for our own freezer. I must say my steak was delicious.

Eating local; in those days, our only option

This is how close our connection was to our food as I was growing up. It seems odd that forty years later, the way my family ate and shopped for food in 1970s rural Northern Ireland comes close to the sustainable lifestyle model many people developed countries desire today.

Our eggs came from the farm next door, our potatoes from "up the road". When our beef was not from our own cattle, it was from the butcher's a few miles away. Top-ups for tea, coffee, biscuits, flour and butter happened at the village shop; and of course in those days, our milk and cream were delivered every morning to our door and we had to remember to bring them in promptly before the blue tits got at the cream through the foil bottle tops.

Supermarket shopping was a monthly occurrence at most, with my father, who had a love of pleasure that was rare in those days, especially for a Presbyterian, steering the trolley through the aisles of food like a child let loose in Father Christmas's workshop. His obsession with the taste of things, the way they were cooked, led to much tension in our kitchen, when, suddenly tyrannical, he would take over the cooking of roasts and steaks to make sure they were "done properly".

Looking back now, I realize how his attitude towards food and the cooking and eating of it, was very French. His absolute sense of entitlement towards the pleasure of good tasting food and lots of it, the obsessive planning of meals, sourcing the ingredients, and the care with which they must be cooked, more than rubbed off on me.

I left all this behind when I escaped (for it was considered escape in those days) Northern Ireland to study in Edinburgh, and found it again when I moved to France in the '80s. An outsider discovering the world's greatest culinary playground, I threw myself into the French love of food and cooking in the days when, as an ambitious working mother, it was completely unfashionable, almost anti-feminist to do so. My new-found French writing career was built on enthusiasm and a palate reared on pure Irish produce, and honed by the world's greatest chefs and, most of all, a keen understanding that *"le ridicule ne tue pas"*.

As I child I had been fully aware of and thankful for the quality of our food at home — it was certainly discussed enough! But those were the worst days of Northern Ireland's conflict, and, like so many of my friends, I longed for a free rein, novelty and fun. The plain and simple food certainly tasted good but to me its simplicity felt acutely like another product of our isolation — both isolation from urban life, as we would rarely venture into Belfast as a family — and the country's isolation from the rest of the world, including the south of Ireland.

Going out in Belfast

It seems crazy now, driving so regularly through Ireland from north to south, that as I grew up, the Republic (referred to as "the Free State" by my maternal grandmother until she died in the '90s) once felt like such a foreign and slightly dangerous place. All I really knew of it were vague, happy memories of Donegal beach holidays as a small child and a couple of (very quick) day trips to Dublin. It took many years away from Ireland for the last traces of that knee-jerk bigotry that a hardline Unionist, Presbyterian upbringing tried to drum into me, to be erased. Thankfully though, natural teenage rebelliousness did not allow me to swallow quite *everything* I heard at home, and this despite an absence of recent Irish history from our school curriculum.

My school was Belfast Royal Academy in the centre of Belfast, and the oldest in the city. In those days, during the height of the Troubles, "town" was somewhere you got in and out of as quickly as possible. Forensically planned shopping trips to Robinson and Cleaver department store (which now houses an excellent restaurant) for our school uniforms, and quick dashes across no-go areas for medical visits were about the height of it. Even on the rare occasions we would eat out with my parents in country hotel carveries on the outskirts of Belfast, usually at lunchtime because evenings were just too risky, we could never fully relax. There were constant bomb scares, roadblocks, army and police checks around the city. No matter how much we willed it to be normal, normal it was not.

Then, when I was 16 or 17, a gaudy, noisy Italian restaurant, Ciro's, opened on Great Victoria Street. To understand what a momentous event this was, you have to imagine a city with no restaurant scene to speak of, where most of the nightlife had been bombed out. I was a teenager whose social life up until then had revolved around school activities and for whom "going out" in the evening meant sneaking, underage, into the odd bar near our farm or being ferried to and from heavily supervised school and church discos. Any exciting eating I had done had been on family holidays abroad to France, Italy, Spain and Greece. At home, the closest I had come to creativity on my plate (apart from my mother's excellent dinner party cooking) was Chicken Maryland in the Beach Hotel, Port Ballintrae (I must go back!).

In hindsight, Ciro's was probably very odd, and the food was probably awful. After all, no one was terribly interested in it back then, but to me it was the most wonderful, wildly exotic place I had come across within Northern Ireland. The atmosphere was electric (I thought) and I loved it dearly. No matter if the half-raw garlic pieces studded through the lasagne would have kept vampires at bay for a week, at last there was somewhere which felt completely different to the everyday and where I could hang out with friends in the centre of town.

Home cooking and hospitality on Horseshoe Farm

In those countryside days, our everyday food at home revolved around bread, milk, bacon, beef and potatoes, with crab apples, strawberries, raspberries, gooseberries and blackberries growing wild, until the hedgerows were slashed back to make room for oilseed rape and silage. For school-day breakfasts we wolfed down toast, fresh milk and bowls of plain cereals (Sugar Puffs as a treat on holidays!) with a very rare (until we learned to make it for ourselves) cooked breakfast on the equally rare Sundays we did not have to walk to Sunday School and then on to church. On weekdays, teas were often fry-ups (in dripping) of sausages, lamb chops, beef steak, liver and bacon with tomatoes and potatoes on the side; quick toasted cheddar and tomatoes on brown pan bread; braised minced beef steak or steak; and kidney in rich onion gravy, again with spuds. On Saturdays, my mother would often boil a ham with cabbage or a "boiler" chicken with two types of soup mix — the first a mix of finely chopped fresh carrots, leek, celery, and parsley; the second — added thirty minutes or so before serving — of orange lentils, barley and split peas.

Naturally, the grandest family meal of the week was lunch on Sunday. If there were guests, we would eat in the dining room on my grandmother's embroidered linen with the good china and crystal and various silver table knick-knacks kept in a special cabinet in the drawing room (which I called "the museum"). We would have fancy starters of smoked salmon, prawn cocktail or Marks & Spencer chicken liver pate, before some invariably magnificent roast beef — cooked rare as my father liked it — with mashed potatoes, carrots and parsnips, gravy and cranberry sauce. Pudding was usually one of my mother's excellent apple tarts, served with milk, cream or ice cream — plain, chocolate or raspberry ripple. (The good stuff came in oblong, fold-back paper packets to be sliced into divots and eaten in thick sandwiches between wafers.)

Rare treats of takeaways, usually fish and chips from nearby Ballynure, were eaten hot in the car (the decadence!) when one of us had done particularly well in our exams and my mother reckoned she had earned an evening off from all her mothering.

Growing up we would have our evening meal around 6 o'clock, after our homework was done. This was "tea", though we would drink milk. Beside our plates there were always bread plates for bread and butter and jam after we had finished the main, and only, course.

On summer holiday on the Antrim Coast, our hotel tea was called High Tea and my parents would leave us to it, waiting another few hours for their more formal dinner.

Those seaside hotel High Teas, taken with the friends we had made at the beach, were wonderful. Not only the main courses were lavish (poached salmon salad! Chicken Maryland and chips!) but the bread was often accompanied by scones, pancakes and fruit cake, and best of all, jelly and ice cream for pudding. It was like a birthday party every evening.

At home, the best high teas were often on Sunday evenings, when the leftovers from the roast were served with pickles, bread and butter and token salads. My favourite was roast lamb, reheated in its gravy, with freshly cooked potatoes and mint sauce served alongside the bread and butter.

Contrasting with the comforting boredom of week-in, week-out cooking, I loved helping out with the rowdy dinner parties my parents would regularly throw for their friends. My mother would try out something new and mildly "continental" from *Good Housekeeping* and, from the age of 11 or so, I was always called in to make dessert of lemon cheesecake, crêpes suzettes or crème caramel. Home baking was a cornerstone of our local community life, with church events, birthday parties, and calls to friends' houses always involving strong tea and tables laden with scones, traybakes, cakes and sandwiches.

Despite its distinct lack of sophistication, our food and its presentation were taken very seriously on Horseshoe Farm, and even more serious still was the ritual and sense of occasion my parents would instill in the different gatherings in our home. As I explained above, it was not easy to circulate in Northern Ireland in those days, and when we did meet up with friends, family or members of the farming community, there was a sort of unspoken recognition of how important it was that we were simply *there*, together.

And this, the getting together, despite the difficulties, is at the heart of Ireland's food culture, all over the island. Through centuries of hardship, famine and war, our simple sharing of good, plain food has taken on and upheld meaning that goes way beyond the mere codes and techniques of cookery.

In ancient Ireland, Irish hospitality (*oigidecht*) was mandated into laws written up in the 7th century by the wandering Brehon judges. They stayed in use until the completion of the English conquest of Ireland in the 17th century and surely explain how a keen sense of hospitality seems to run in our blood. According to Brehon law, only children, old people and madmen were exempt from welcoming any stranger into their home and providing them with food and shelter with no questions asked. This generosity promoted trade and travel and no payment was allowed, excepting in the form of a story, a song or a poem, and only then once the traveller had availed themselves of the free hospitality. Quite simply, wealth was shown by how much you could give, not how much you possessed, and anyone who failed to provide an adequate welcome was fined, regardless of their level in society.

The tradition of an open door to strangers, a cup of tea ("a drop in yer hand" as we say up north) or a glass of whiskey with a bite to eat is still deeply ingrained in Ireland's culture. It is this I missed most during my years living in France's gastronomic paradise, and this, I think, which brought me back to Ireland to write the book you hold in your hands.

Irish food: from a traumatic heritage to a vibrant new culture

Until the 1960s, the English conquest and Great Famines of the mid-17th century and 1840s were the two main factors which had shaped Ireland's food culture. For centuries before the English colonisation and the disastrous failure of the potato crop, Ireland was a country rich with game and fish, whose temperate climate and fertile soil made for excellent tillage and livestock farming. English control of Ireland's natural resources led to farms being divided into ever smaller holdings and a disastrous over-reliance on the seemingly miraculous potato, introduced from the New World in the 17th century. By the 1840s, Ireland's population had grown to over eight million, but by the end of the century, over a million had died of starvation and twice as many had fled the country, greatly contributing to the immense Irish diaspora we know today.

The notion of food as a sociable or physical pleasure during the years of recovery after the famines was a difficult one for the Irish to assimilate, as was the idea of an indigenous fine cuisine. For the ordinary people living on the land, food meant survival, and growing sufficient amounts was a prerequisite to regaining control of their farms. In those days there were only two "twists" on native Irish dishes — enough or not enough.

It's interesting to contrast post-famine Ireland with late 19th century France, which, from the release of the nobility's cooks across the country after the revolution, was enjoying the creation of restaurants and an explosion of actively egalitarian pleasurable eating, made possible by a fabulously rich and varied national *terroir*. Their wonderful cooking soon spread outside France and influenced English and Irish cooking as much as it did many parts of the world.

For most of the 19th and 20th centuries, bourgeois dining centred around French and "big house" English-style dishes, and until Theodora Fitzgibbon's seminal *Irish Traditional Food* (Gill and Macmillan, 1983), the Irish cooking catalogued in cookbooks of the last century was practically interchangeable with English. True Irish recipes had little attention paid to them.

But the general disinterest in Irish food culture, tinged with a squeamishness and rejection of "famine food", started to fade from the 1970s onwards, after Mrs Myrtle Allen opened a groundbreaking restaurant in her husband's family home, Ballymaloe House near Shanagarry in East Cork. Years before Alice Waters' Chez Panisse in California, Mrs Allen cooked simple, seasonal dishes with the food grown on her farm and on the lands around it, and fished and hunted from woodlands and sea nearby. Myrtle Allen's daughter-in-law Darina has since become one of the world's most respected campaigners for sustainable food production, having created the renowned Ballymaloe Cookey school with her brother Rory O'Connell. Food writers and experts in Ireland's food history, including Biddy White Lennon, Georgina Campbell, Sally and John McKenna and of course Theodora FitzGibbon, have also greatly contributed to the broadening of knowledge of Ireland's food over the past decades and have heralded a new confidence in our native Irish produce and how to cook it.

Fast forward to 2015, and post Celtic Tiger, super tech-savvy Ireland has caught right up with the rest of the world as it goes crazy for food. Thanks to the internet and cheap airfares, the nation has become fluent in the language of food as aspirational lifestyle, status symbol or fashion statement. Our appetite for world trends in restaurants is as large as that of any other developed country and we have even started a few trends of our own — with Belfast twins Gary and Alan Keery opening the Cereal Killers café in Shoreditch, London, and a pair of crisp sandwich cafés (Simply Crispy) following hard on its heels in Belfast and Dublin.

Even our "famine food" has come full circle, with reflected light shone on it by Rene Redzepi's Nordic cuisine revolution, elevating our edible reminders of harsh times — root vegetables, grains, seafood, game, seaweeds, wild berries — to gourmet status while at the same time shrinking them, ironically, into molecular micro portions on the plate. Likewise, our ancient techniques of brewing, pickling, and smoking are right on trend all over the world, from US foodies' Mecca, Portland, to super cool Melbourne via gastronomic heavyweight Tokyo.

Artisan cheesemaking, baking, distilling and brewing are areas which have perhaps seen the most progress over the past decade, and are leading the way in winning back customers disillusioned with industrially manufactured produce.

All around Ireland, from the smallest store to the largest supermarket, quality Irish produce is invading the shelves. In between, food halls like Fallon and Byrne in Dublin and Ardkeen in Waterford are championing Irish produce more and more in a country where it seems the best has always been exported.

Farmers' markets are thriving, with a few, like those at Midleton and Mahon Point, choosing stallholders according to strict criteria. Adhering to self-imposed sustainable andst organic guidelines, they are resisting the tacos, pizzas and candyfloss stalls to provide a real alternative to consumers, offering more than just an afternoon out or a venue for a lively lunch-on-the-hoof.

No pistachios or pomegranates were harmed in the making of this book

It is a fascinating time for Irish food. We are at a crossroads between old and new, innovation and tradition. Everywhere across Ireland, for better for worse, completely unreconstructed restaurants, chip shops and pubs sit next to groovy places serving great pizza or terrific coffee. We have embraced fusion, regularly declaring "modern Irish" to be any number of internationally inspired culinary "takes" on our fantastic native produce.

In the 100 addresses in the annexes of this book, I have pointed you to some of the best places to eat out and shop for food in Ireland, but *these* pages are all about cooking at home. What interested me was to go back to our home-cooked basics, to new and old dishes using the main ingredients Irish people grew and produced for centuries before the famine years — potatoes, oats, cabbage, mutton, bacon, stout, milk and cream. Of course our cuisine has been through transformations, as is the case in any country that has been regularly invaded during its history. The Anglo-Normans in the 12th and 13th centuries, and then the Elizabethans and Jacobites, brought with them many spices, including ginger, aniseed, mace and cloves. More exotic fruits like oranges and peaches were enjoyed by rich 18th century landowners who had the means to cultivate a variety of fruit and vegetables in their glasshouses and import rarer ingredients such as chocolate and vanilla, but they were inaccessible to most of the population.

I have included many favourites from my childhood, many wonderful creations and versions of classics from friends' kitchens, and a good number of traditional recipes such as Coddle, Colcannon or Irish Stew (but not all of them). At the same time, in full-on "returning native" mode, as a creative limitation in which to frame the collection, and, most of all, just to show it can be done, I have resisted the Southern European, Middle Eastern and American influences and ingredients currently so fashionable, and have avoided simply substituting Irish ingredients into a foreign dish and calling it "Irish". With such an abundance of fabulous new Irish produce, these have been easy, delicious and super-creative

Sunday evening high tea.

limitations to work within. It felt like I was being handed a brand new palette of colours, a dictionary full of words that had been left aside for a while and were now being dusted off to be used once again.

In attempting to think up new ways of associating our native culinary produce, I've used broths and juices, seaweed, pickles and raw vegetables but have still rejoiced in the pure taste of our cream, butter, bread and potatoes.

As ever, my recipes are extremely simple, requiring very few ingredients and minimal space or equipment. I believe that a great part of the beauty and appeal of Irish cooking lies precisely in that very simplicity, and I want everyone to have a go, and, hopefully, end up adding a few Irish dishes to their weekly routine. The recipes are aimed at beginner cooks or those like me who are merely lazy, but there is also a smattering of brilliant, exquisitely presented chefs' food, by the chefs themselves, photographed in their restaurants, for the hardcore gastro-curious among you to try. There are also many contributions, in the form of recipes and stories, from some of the food loving people I've met along the way.

Home

I think it is being away from Ireland for so long that has made me Irish, not British as I was born. In Ireland an Irish man or woman will be placed to within about five miles of their home town as soon as they open their mouth, and there's a hundred subliminal historic labels attached to their accent. Most French people, however, see us as one nation, on one island, and make very little distinction between an Irish man or woman from West or East, North or South. Over the years this has had an effect on me and I think, all things considered, I may have come to agree with them.

My travels home over the past six or seven years have been through a very different Ireland from the one in which I grew up. Not only did I see the transformation of Belfast and Northern Ireland, I've had a lot of my childhood suspicions confirmed about the fun and warmth and damn good time to be had. Travelling has created a sort of retrospective nostalgia for a fantasy land (Pete McCarthy writes about "genetic memory" in his memoir, *McCarthy's Bar*) and its living, lively culture that, miraculously, has turned out to be real. A truly comforting, nourishing feeling after so many years living in France.

I saw too that the land, sea and rain, and the food they grow for us, all over the country, envelop us in the same way, and unite us much more than divide when it comes to what is on our plates and the way we eat it. Local variations on themes abound — how many recipes for brown, soda or wheaten bread can there be in Ireland? Or for potato scones, farls or Fadge? The familiarity and repetition of what we fed each other, the barely perceptible variations in an Irish stew, a scone, a cup of tea, or a slice of tea brack, from one kitchen to another, was an elemental fuel that bound us and, as it lives on and evolves, binds us still.

From one end of the country to the other, our original culinary repertoire is a simple but powerful one, cooked from a shared heart and a homegrown larder with a couple of dozen core ingredients. It is alive and thriving, and this book is, I hope, a celebration of it.

It has taken almost half my life away from Ireland for me to truly *feel* what home really is, and it is not what I was expecting. In the end it was not a place, or a past, or any sort of single, dazzling epiphany. It was all the little things. Cold butter spread thick on sweet wheaten bread or hot, subsiding potatoes; the scent of wet, black soil; a bushy spine of grass on a one-track road; wide iron gates leading to high beech corridors; the chalky smell of a cow's wet muzzle, and, most of all, in Seamus Heaney's words, the sound of rivers in the trees.

OATS, POTATOES, KALE AND CABBAGE

Potato harvest, Standing Stone Farm, Doagh, Co. Antrim.

PROPER PORRIDGE

Gone are the memories of the gloopy, bland hotel breakfast mush, served in dubious-looking black vats, which put me off porridge for so many years. When I finally discovered the nutty taste and comforting bite of "proper" porridge, a few years ago in Dublin, I was hooked. Where had it been all my life?

There are quite a few forms of oats available, though very often we do not get past the packet with the jolly looking chap in the big black hat. That's a shame, because these are rolled oats — cut grains which have been steamed and flattened — and their taste and texture are incomparable to steel-cut pinhead — whole grains simply cut in two which need soaking before cooking — or oatmeal which is made by grinding whole grains to coarse, medium or fine consistency.
Jumbo oats are the most frowned upon by porridge purists. These are the whole grains, steamed and flattened for fast cooking; quickly leaving you with a pappy gunge.

Rolled and jumbo oats are very convenient of course, cooking quickly and easily as porridge and into our granolas, cookies and energy bars. But for a really good bowl of porridge, try mixing oatmeal with steel-cut pinhead oats. This gives a little bite and masses of taste.

The Scots swear by water and salt for their austere porridge. I much prefer half-fat milk, though a pinch of salt, even under a layer of sugar, brings out the taste beautifully. For the perfect bowl, you should toast the oats before cooking. Though for many this is too much like hard work early in the morning when you need your fix.

Serve with dried or fresh fruit, nuts, yoghurt, cream, honey or golden syrup. It is a fantastic base for a nutritious breakfast that will keep you fuelled until lunchtime.

For 1
15 minutes cooking
3 to 5 minutes resting

25 g pinhead oatmeal (soaked for a few hours or overnight and drained)
25 g medium oatmeal
200 ml half-fat milk
Pinch of salt
Demerara sugar
Cream, honey or golden syrup

Put the milk into a non-stick saucepan and bring to the boil.

Tip in the oats, turn the heat down and simmer very gently for about 15 minutes, stirring often.
The oatmeal will be very soft. The steel-cut grains will still have some pop and bite to them.

Take the porridge off the heat and let it rest for up to 5 minutes — it will be too hot to eat right away! — before serving just the way you like it, though perhaps not with QUITE as much cream as in the photo.

SAVOURY PORRIDGE WITH HEGARTY'S CHEDDAR AND CRISPY SAGE

I'm not sure if it could ever take off, this idea of switching sweet for savoury in our sacred national porridge. Eating it at breakfast, for me anyway, has so much more to do with simple sustenance, comfort and convenience than creating any kind of "dish." It is the ultimate mood food and, at 7 am, let's face it, my mood is pretty grim.

Taking two off-white ingredients, stirring them gently with a wooden spoon, adjusting their plainness with something sweet and, possibly, adding something creamy, is just about as much cooking as I like to do in the morning, at least until the coffee has hit home. But grains are so very good for you, and since oats have not been spared the irresistible food trend limelight, I was keen to try something different. Here's a non-sweet way of cooking them, which could, at a pinch, provide a nice bed for some fried bacon if you happen to be cooking a fancy breakfast or brunch. This cheesy porridge is also excellent as a warming winter starter or as a side with veal or pork chops. You could swap the sage for parsley if it's hard to get hold of. Hegarty's cheddar, a traditional cloth-bound cheddar made using pasteurised cow's milk and vegetarian rennet is made near Whitechurch in North Cork.

For 4
25 minutes cooking

175 g porridge oats
500 ml fresh, half-fat milk
100 g good Irish cheddar (Wicklow, Hegartys, Coolattin)
100 ml fresh, single cream
20 or so fresh sage leaves
125 g butter

First, prepare the sage leaves. Put some kitchen paper on a plate. It's for draining the sage once it's cooked.

Melt the butter in a small saucepan, then heat it until it simmers. Add the sage leaves, 4 or 5 at a time, letting them bubble and fry until they are crispy and slightly golden around the edges.

Remove them from the butter with a fork or a small slotted spoon and set them on the kitchen paper to drain and dry. You can season them with a very fine dusting of salt if you like.

Bring the oats and the milk to the boil. Reduce the heat and cook, stirring all the while until the porridge is soft, but still has a slight bite.

Take the saucepan off the heat and crumble or grate the cheese into the hot porridge, mixing it through to melt it. Season, salt and pepper. Put the porridge into four bowls, add the cream in an enticing swirl, top with the sage leaves and serve at once.

A field of oats near Baltimore, Co. Cork.

EGGY, BACON-Y, MUSHROOMY OATS

It has all the breakfast things, but again, this is not a last-minute-scramble-to-get-out-the-door type of recipe. It's more for weekend brunches or weekday suppers. Add spinach, kale, scallions, onions, potatoes, and all sorts of meltable cheese to make it even more interesting. And poach that egg, if you prefer, for even more softness. I guess it's only a matter of time before someone will want to put an avocado on there too...

For 1
3 minutes preparation
20 minutes cooking

50 g pinhead oatmeal
350 ml (approximately, you may need slightly more or less) vegetable or ham stock. Water will do but then perhaps add a scallion to the mushrooms.
3 to 4 button mushrooms, or anything fancier like ceps, chanterelles, parasols or hedgehogs you may have found or foraged, sliced
20 g butter
2 rashers of good, free range bacon, cut into 1 cm pieces
1 egg
50 g good Irish cheddar
3 to 4 cherry tomatoes, split in two

Heat the stock and tip in the oats when it comes to the boil. Lower the heat and simmer for about 20 minutes, stirring regularly while you prepare the rest of the dish. Top up with water if the porridge dries out.

Heat the butter in a frying pan, slice the mushrooms and fry them with the bacon bits until golden and crispy. Keep the mushrooms and bacon warm.

When the oats are cooked, season lightly and leave to cool. While they are cooling, fry the egg.

Serve the oats in a bowl with the mushrooms and bacon bits stirred through it, and the egg, tomatoes and grated cheese on top.

SWEDE AND CARROT BAKED WITH OATS AND CHEDDAR

This simple twist to the usual mashed swede and carrots, can make it into a quick, standalone weekday supper or as a jazzed-up accompaniment to meat, pork and lamb.

For 6
5 minutes preparation
45 minutes cooking

450 g carrots, peeled, roughly chopped
450 g swedes, peeled, roughly chopped
40 g butter
2 eggs
50 ml fresh milk

Salt and pepper
75 g porridge oats
50 g good cheddar, freshly grated

Pre-heat the oven to 190 °C and butter a medium-sized gratin dish.

Steam or boil the carrot and swede together until tender. Mash the vegetables with the eggs, half the butter and milk and season with salt and pepper.

Put the mash into the dish and sprinkle the oats and cheese on top.

Bake for 25 minutes or so, until the oats and cheese are toasted.

SWEET BAKED OATS

A sort of comforting, creamy, nutty, oaty pudding and now a regular at my breakfast table. It's a practical and rather luxurious way of serving four or more without continually re-doing pots of fresh porridge. With more cream for pouring and fresh or poached fruit (or perhaps a nip of whiskey?) it's a simple suppertime pudding. Sliced, dipped in beaten egg and fried in butter it's also pretty delicious in leftovers form.

For 6
10 minutes preparation
25 minutes cooking

225 g medium oatmeal
1 teaspoon baking powder
1 teaspoon ground mace (or mixed spice)
A pinch of salt
150 g hazelnuts, roughly crushed
325 ml fresh whole milk
175 ml double cream
75 g Irish honey
75 g brown sugar
1 large egg

Toast the hazelnuts in a frying pan and leave to cool.

Pre-heat the oven to 180 °C. Butter a 20 cm x 20 cm gratin or ovenproof dish.

Mix the oats with the baking powder, salt, ground mace and cooled toasted nuts. Put the mixture into the dish.

Whisk the cream, milk, honey, sugar and egg together and pour this sweet custard over the oats. Sprinkle a little more sugar over the top.

Bake until the oats are golden on top and the custard has completely soaked into them (for about 25 minutes). The oats will continue soaking up the custard so don't worry at this stage if it looks a little runny.

Remove from the oven and leave to cool slightly, before serving with poached fruit, cream, buttermilk or ice cream.

STANDING STONE FARM, DOAGH, CO. ANTRIM

The potatoes are teased from the cool, rich soil of Wilbert Robinson's fields before being shifted into crates in his enormous barns and delivered across Northern Ireland. Standing Stone Farm is in the Six Mile Water Valley, near Doagh, below the Holestone, a bronze age megalith just a stone's throw from the farm where I grew up. It was used for pagan betrothals, and it's still an unlikely romantic spot today, sitting high amongst gorse bushes in County Antrim farmlands.

The history of potatoes in Ireland is far from romantic. *Solanum tubersporum* will forever be associated with death and the unspeakable hardship ordinary Irish people encountered in the 1840s, when Ireland's population was halved due to emigration and death from starvation as the potato crops failed. Over a million fled the country in an attempt to survive. But hardier varieties than the ill-fated Lumper (grown then because of its high yield and now being slowly reintroduced to Ireland) were developed, and today potatoes are still a huge part of the traditional Irish diet. Every year the arrival of the crops of new potatoes in May, June and July is still an important time in our kitchens. The months between the end of the old crop and the first new praties were the most difficult ones to survive for many years in Ireland.

In Northern Ireland, the smooth and nutty new season Comber potatoes or "Comber Earlies" were awarded Protected Geographical Indication (PGI) status under European law. One of only three products in Northern Ireland (and five in the Republic) to be granted the distinction, along with Lough Neagh Eels, and Armagh Bramleys.

Even if it's now rarer for modern restaurants to serve the four or five types of spuds I was often offered when eating out with my parents as a child (boiled, sautéed, creamed or mashed, chipped, roast or "croquette"), potatoes are still firmly on the menu at home, and you'll find them for sale out of horse trucks by the roadside, in corner stores, and taking up metres of aisles in every supermarket. The new season potatoes now have their very own festivals!

In Ireland, we like our spuds fluffy and floury, as it makes it easier to soak up butter, gravy or whatever stew or soup is sitting alongside. These perfect sauce cushions are best steamed, and over-boiling is a constant hazard in Irish kitchens. Many's a time the cook returns to the pot to find limp skins floating in pasty white water.

Maris Piper are most popular for chips, Roosters and Kerr's Pink with their white to pink skins and cream flesh are the two biggest selling varieties grown, with Queens also popular from late June to September.

As well as those grown for large scale production, there are dozens of lesser known Irish varieties. Many of them, such as Orla and Duke of York, are more suitable for smaller gardens and home-growing. Two of Ireland's food heroes, gardener Dermot Carey and potato grower and collector Dave Langford, are helping lead Ireland's potato revival. Dermot was head gardener at Harry's walled garden in Bridgend and then at Lissadell Estate, where he oversaw the arrival of Dave Langford's extensive potato collection — over 190 varieties!

Wilbert Robinson on Standing Stone farm, Doagh Co. Antrim.

CHAMP

Champ, which is made with mashed potatoes, butter, milk and chopped spring onions (scallions) or leeks, was a dish in its own right centuries ago in Ireland, often served with scrambled eggs in its centre, according to Theodora Fitzgibbon. The potatoes were cooked in iron pots over open fires and crushed with a beetle, a large wooden masher which looks a little like a wooden skittle.

Nowadays, it is as popular as ever, but tends to accompany meat dishes, and is especially good with Beef in Guinness. Champ was often on my grandmother's table and in our school dinner hall, growing up. And even if I preferred my spuds plain — blue, floury and falling apart in their skins on my plate — I did love playing with the butter volcano in the centre of a pile of champ, drawing the drier potato from the sides to dip in it before it sank away into the fluffiness.

The usual recipe calls for scallions to be soaked in hot milk, but when they are fresh, pale green and very tender they are deliciously crunchy, simply chopped and mixed into the mash potato at the last minute. You can also add chives, parsley, nettles or fresh peas poached in milk.

For 4 to 6
10 minutes preparation
20 to 25 minutes cooking

650 g floury potatoes, peeled and cut into chunks
5 to 6 spring onions, finely sliced
250 ml fresh milk
100 g salted butter
Salt and pepper

Simmer the scallions in the milk for about 5 minutes. Drain and reserve the milk. Boil the potatoes in salted water for 20 to 25 minutes until they are tender.

Mash the potatoes with the milk and about 25 g of butter until they are creamy. Season with salt and pepper, add the scallions and stir them through the potatoes. Make a volcano shaped pile in the plates and pop the rest of the butter in the craters. Serve immediately.

NETTLE CHAMP

Chop a couple of handfuls of fresh nettle tops and poach in the 250 ml of boiling milk for 1-2 minute.

Then make the champ the replacing the scallions with the nettles.

POTATO RAVIOLI WITH LEEK BY DAVID HURLEY, GREGAN'S CASTLE HOTEL

"This dish takes a classic combination of potato and leek, with the use of different textures and preparations. It makes for, I hope, a pleasant and interesting eating experience. There is the silky-smooth potato puree in the ravioli sitting on top of a diced potato and leek salad, offset with a fried potato crisp, creamy leek velouté and onion cress. Both the filling and the pasta dough need to be prepared a couple of hours in advance, but once this is done the ravioli can be made and refrigerated for up to 24 hours before cooking at the very last minute."

For 8
45 minutes preparation
2 hours resting the pasta
5 minutes cooking

For the pasta
250 g '00' pasta flour
1 whole egg
4 egg yolks
2 tablespoon milk
1 tablespoon olive oil
1 teaspoon vinegar
Good pinch salt

For the filling
300 g baking potatoes
175 g cream
75 g butter
Salt and pepper

For the pasta, place all the ingredients in a bowl and mix to a rough dough. Remove from the bowl and knead for 10 minutes until smooth and elastic. Refrigerate for a couple of hours before using.

Place the baking potatoes on a baking tray and bake at 180 °C for about 1 hour depending on size, or until a small knife can easily pierce the center. Remove the potatoes from the oven and cut in half, scoop out the flesh and discard the skins.

Heat the cream and place in a food processor with the hot potato and diced butter. Season and blend until smooth. Transfer to a container and refrigerate until set.

Scoop out the potato mix with a spoon into desired sizes. Try to scoop it to form a nice rounded shape for the raviolo. Place on a tray in the fridge to keep firm.

Roll out the pasta very thinly in small batches, ideally with a pasta machine, keeping the remaining dough covered with a damp cloth, only lightly flouring, as the pasta dough will dry out and become too brittle to work with otherwise.

Sandwich the potato filling between 2 pieces of rolled pasta dough dampened lightly with water, carefully ensuring all air has been removed to avoid the raviolo bursting open when cooking.

The best way of keeping these until needed is to refrigerate them on a plate lined with fine polenta, this will prevent them sticking and is easily removed before cooking.

Cook the ravioli in simmering salted water for 2-3 min depending on how you like your pasta cooked. Remove from the water and brush with melted butter.

POTATO
APPLE STUFFING

In Ireland the Christmas goose is stuffed, traditionally, with this simple, herby mashed potato mix.
It's also terrific with chicken or in rolled, stuffed pork loin. Nowadays, thanks to our hygienically
challenged food production system, the stuffing is almost always cooked separately from the bird. Some say
this is an improvement, not a loss, as the meat retains the juices, which would have soaked into the bread.
In Florence Irwin's *The Cookin' Woman* she gives a recipe for "Mock Goose": a pig's stomach — given in
olden days to one of the farm labourers when a pig was killed — was cleaned out with a hard brush, salted,
rinsed well, "loosely filled with potato and onion stuffing" sewn up and roasted for 2-3 hours in lard in a pot
oven with fire embers set on top.
Potato Pudding is another one of many old, traditional "pratie" dishes to be found throughout Ireland.
Usually eaten at Halloween, mashed potatoes were kneaded with flour, seasoned and sweetened, before
being rolled out and baked with milk in a pot oven over the fire for at least 4 hours. Flavourings varied from
county to county, with apples, eggs, spices and butter being mixed and matched to give infinite versions.

For 6
25 minutes preparation
60 minutes cooking (separately from the goose)

5 or 6 medium potatoes
75 g butter
1 onion, finely chopped
2 cooking apples, peeled, grated
Fresh sage, thyme, parsley
Salt and pepper

Boil or steam the potatoes until they are tender but still firm. Sweat the onions in a little butter without
colouring them.

Mash the potatoes with the rest of the butter. Add the onions, grated apples and fresh herbs and season
with salt and pepper.

Stuff the goose or cook the stuffing alongside it for an hour or so before it is ready to serve.

CREAM OF POTATO SOUP WITH HAZELNUT AND WILD GARLIC PESTO

Super simple to make and serve. The pesto will keep up to a week in the fridge and is great with grilled meats and fish. Use young, blanched nettles instead of, or mixed into, the wild garlic, to add a lovely grassy note to the pesto.

For 4
10 minutes preparation
30 minutes cooking

4 to 6 large fluffy potatoes, peeled, chopped into chunks
500 ml chicken or vegetable stock
2 large onions, finely chopped
50 g butter
Salt and pepper
200 ml fresh cream
150 g hazelnuts
1 good handful of wild garlic leaves
Rapeseed oil

Bring the stock to the boil and simmer the potatoes in it until they are tender and fluffy.

Sweat the onions gently in a frying pan with a little butter until they soften, without colouring them.

Add them to the potatoes and liquidize with a handheld mixer or in a food processor. Add the cream and season to taste.

Whizz the hazelnuts and wild garlic (and blanched nettles if you are using them) in a mini processor with some oil — you want the past to have a ketchup-like looseness — and season.

Serve the hot soup in bowls, swirled with the pesto and a little more cream if you fancy it.

NETTLE AND SODA BREAD CRUMB PESTO FOR SOUPS

For 4
10 minutes cooking

100 g young nettles
1 thick slice of day-old soda or wheaten bread, toasted, broken into chunks
30 g or so of good Irish cheddar
150 ml rapeseed oil
Salt and pepper

Bring a pan of water to the boil. Push the nettles in — wearing gloves! — and blanch for a minute or so. Drain thoroughly. In a mini processor, put the bread, nettles, cheese and some oil. Whizz to a loose consistency, adding more oil as you need it. Season and use in soup or savoury porridge, or as a dip with drinks.

BOXTY

"Boxty on the griddle, boxty on the pan; if you can't make boxty, you'll never get a man" goes the old Irish rhyme. And this is one of those "famous", traditional Irish potato dishes so often trotted out for St Patrick's Day around the world yet not terribly easy to find in Ireland. Boxty would generally not be on the menu of today's busy households or date night menus and I have rarely found it as pub grub.
It is a great way of using up leftover mash by mixing it with crunchy, freshly grated potato and making it all into crisp pancakes. Make Boxty in a heavy based pan if you don't have a griddle like mine, and feel free to add onion, seaweed, bacon or fresh herbs, or all of those things, if you like.

This recipe follows quite closely Biddy White Lennon's, one of Ireland's best known and loved food writers (and the Irish counterpart of Mary Berry in the Great Irish Bake Off!).

For 6 to 8 farls
20 minutes preparation
30 minutes cooking

250 g peeled raw potatoes
250 g hot mashed potato (cooked)
250 g plain flour
½ teaspoon baking powder
75 g melted butter
Fresh milk or buttermilk to bind
Salt and pepper

Grate the raw potatoes onto a clean tea towel.

Lift the edges of the cloth and twist them over the potatoes to make a tight ball in the middle.
Wring the cloth by twisting the edges and gather the liquid from the potatoes in a bowl.

Put the wrung-out potatoes in a bowl and cover them with the hot mashed potato. This stops the raw potato discolouring.

The potato liquid will settle, with the whiter starch dropping to the bottom.

Pour off the clear water and mix the starch into the grated and mashed potatoes (I leave this bit out when I'm too impatient). Add the melted butter and stir well.

Sift the flour and baking powder into the potato with a good pinch of salt and pepper and mix again well.

Pour a little milk or buttermilk into the boxty, bring it together with your hands and knead it for a minute or so until the dough is supple.

Cut it in two, roll out two circles and cut them into triangles.

Cook on a heated griddle or in a non-stick pan. Biddy bakes hers in the oven at 180 °C for 30 minutes or so.

Eat hot and buttered.

COLCANNON

Made of mashed potatoes with spring onions (scallions) — food writer Theodora FitzGibbon used leeks or onion tops for hers — and softened cabbage or kale, Colcannon is from the Irish *cál ceannann*, meaning "white-headed cabbage" and was traditionally served up at Halloween, with charms hidden in the dish.

According to Theodora: "A plain gold ring, a sixpence, a thimble or a button are often put into the mixture. The ring means you'll be married within the year, the sixpence denotes wealth, the thimble a spinster and the button a bachelor, to whoever gets them."

For 4
20 minutes preparation
25 minutes cooking

2 kg floury potatoes
1 head of green cabbage or kale
250 ml fresh milk or cream, or a mix of the two
125 g butter
4 or 5 scallions
Salt and pepper

Peel the potatoes and put them in a large pot of cold water to boil.

Slice the cabbage thinly, or if you are using kale remove the inner stalk and slice the leafy parts thinly. Put the cabbage or kale into a saucepan, cover it with boiling water from the kettle and let it simmer slowly for 4 or 5 minutes until it is wilted and softened.

Drain the cabbage well, squeezing it to remove any excess moisture. Put it back in the saucepan with about a third of the butter and give it a swirl around so it becomes nicely coated. Cover the pan to keep the cabbage or kale warm while you are attending to the potatoes.

When the potatoes are tender, drain them well and put them back in the pot on the heat, again to remove as much moisture as possible.

Warm the milk with the chopped scallions and pour it onto the potatoes. Mash with a fork or a potato masher, but do not overdo it or the Colcannon will become sticky.

Mix the cabbage or kale through the potatoes with a light hand.

Season with salt and pepper, make a mound in the centre of the plate with a well for the rest of the butter in the middle.

Signpost to the Dillisk Food Project, a summer pop-up in Aughrusbeg, Connemara.

CABBAGE AND POTATO SOUP WITH TOASTED, BUTTERED SODA CRUMBS AND SUGAR KELP

The most banal and common ingredients get a bit of a revamp in this warming, thrifty soup thanks to the seaweed's umami notes and the buttery crunch of the soda farl. As ever, I prefer plain water to inferior stock, so the "optional" in the ingredients list refers to that. Please do not resort to industrial stock cubes or powder, they will ruin the taste and fill you with evil chemicals. Besides, the vegetables here are all so flavourful; if anything, using water will tone down their earthiness and leave room for the seaweed to do its stuff. And sorry if 125 g of butter seems a lot, you can of course reduce that, but please do not leave it out completely — cabbage and potatoes will always cry out for it.

For 4
10 minutes preparation
25 minutes cooking

About half a cabbage, green or white, chopped roughly
2 onions, peeled and chopped
3 or 4 nice floury potatoes (about 600 g) peeled, cut in quarters
A couple of sticks of celery, plus leaves, chopped roughly
2 tablespoons (or equivalent in a sprig) fresh flat-leaf parsley
100 g butter
1 tablespoon vegetable oil
1 litre vegetable or chicken stock (optional)
Salt and pepper
1 white or wheaten soda farl
2 tablespoons Broughgammon Farm dried sugar kelp flakes (or another dried seaweed you might prefer)

In a good, heavy, wide-based saucepan, melt 30 g of butter with the oil and sweat the onions, without colouring them, for a minute or two. Add the cabbage, potatoes and celery and, on a low heat, let them all sweat and soften together for about 5 more minutes. When they are nicely softened, cover the vegetables with boiling water or stock, season lightly with salt and pepper, bring the saucepan to the boil and leave to simmer for about 20 minutes, or until the potatoes are soft and starting to break up.

Heat 50 g of butter in a frying pan and crumble the soda farl into the pan, letting it toast and brown in the hot butter until it becomes nicely browned. Set aside and keep warm (in the pan is fine, and good for a quick warming blast of heat just as you are serving the soup).

When the vegetables are soft, remove the pan from the heat and blitz the soup in a blender or with a hand-held cousin. I much prefer the latter, though do be careful not to burn yourself with the inevitable splashes.

Add the seaweed and stir it through with the remaining butter. Only then adjust the seasoning of the soup, as the seaweed is salty! Garnish with parsley, if you're using it, and the soda crumbs, and serve.

STEPHEN TOMAN

Chef STEPHEN TOMAN trained at Taillevent and L'Astrance in Paris, and if his cooking is influenced by world restaurant trends it certainly doesn't ape them, instead championing Northern Irish ingredients in a modern and accessible style. In Ireland, the awards are already raining down on this cool, calm young man. With wooden tables, no tablecloths, and a long, cushioned bench along its main wall, OX's industrial feel is more soft warehouse than gritty machine room. Stevie's cooking heralds the emergence of a new, modern Irishness, and here our best produce is in world-class, capable, caring hands. There is no botanical overdose of foraged herbs or flower power at OX, no overuse of foams or Pacojet purées so popular in many gastro bistros. Bushmills whiskey, Lough Neagh eel and Skeaghamore duck sit alongside other fine local ingredients, sourced directly from the farm. The accent is firmly on conviviality and, despite the keen gastronomic originality on the plate, manager Alain Kerloc'h (who trained at Alain Passard in Paris and founded Mirazur in Menton with Mauro Cologreco) is ultra concerned that customers' experience of a meal at OX should be relaxing and welcoming. There is no asking for tables back at 10 pm here; guests can spend as long as they want sampling the sparkling menu, and then move next door to OX Cave wine bar to prolong the evening still further.

HAY BAKED CELERIAC, BLACK GARLIC, SORREL, BURNT ONION BY STEVIE TOMAN, OX BELFAST

For 8
20 minutes preparation
3 hours cooking

2 onions
1 celeriac
2 or 3 handfuls fresh hay
50 g black garlic
2 egg yolks
1 teaspoon white wine vinegar
200 ml vegetable oil
Salt and pepper
Bunch of sorrel
Gourmet salt
Good quality rapeseed oil

Peel and thinly slice the onion, roast in hot oven at 200 °C for 5 minutes until it browns.

Lower heat to 100 °C for a further 10 minutes to dry out. Allow to cool and blitz in spice grinder until a fine powder.

Wrap the whole celeriac in hay in a deep casserole dish then cover with tinfoil and bake in oven at 180 °C for 3-4 hours until core temperature is 94 °C (use a probe to test this).

Leave to rest for 15-20 minutes before carving.

Whisk egg yolk and vinegar, slowly adding oil, to make a mayonnaise. Puree the mayonnaise with black garlic in a blender, pass through a fine sieve and season with salt.

Dust onion powder onto hot plate, peel the celeriac with knife and cut into thick rectangles, season with gourmet salt, and pepper, spoon on a few dots of black garlic, garnish with sorrel leaves and drizzle with rapeseed oil.

SCALLION, CELERY AND PARSLEY SOUP

Three good, green things you will find in every Irish store, no matter how small, all year round. No need for extra stock, these are three mightily robust flavours on their own. Made with a bit of love, laced with a bit of butter (and cream if you fancy), served with soda bread, it's a cheap and wholesome supper that's ready in no time. Add some pearl barley and lentils to beef it up even more as it simmers.

For 4
10 minutes preparation
25 minutes cooking

1 head of celery
4 or 5 scallions (spring onions)
A good handful of parsley
50 g butter
A splash of cream
Salt and pepper

Wash and finely chop the scallions, celery and half of the sprig of parsley.

In a heavy bottomed pan, sweat the ingredients together in the butter, without browning, until they start to soften. Add enough water to comfortably cover the vegetables. Bring to the boil and then simmer gently for 20 to 25 minutes until the celery is soft.

Take the pan off the heat and blitz the soup with a hand held blender. Season with salt and pepper, add butter and cream to taste and serve piping hot and fresh.

BROTCHAN ROY

The name means "A broth fit for a king", but Irish broth, or brotchan, was made by Irish peasants with oatmeal and vegetables long before any royally luxurious meat was added to the pot. Leeks and nettles were often used, adding taste and nutrition to this thick soup.

450 ml water, milk beef or vegetable stock
25 g porridge oats
1 leek, washed and chopped
25 g butter, lard or beef dripping
A pinch of ground mace
Chopped parsley for serving
Salt and pepper

Heat the fat in the bottom of a large saucepan and fry the oats until they are golden. Add the chopped leeks with the mace, some salt and pepper, cook for a minute or so, then pour in the liquid.

Bring to the boil and simmer for 30 to 40 minutes. Serve hot with the parsley garnish.

KALE CHIPS WITH RAPESEED OIL, SALT AND DEMERARA SUGAR

This is not a nod to hipsterdom. Kale has been growing in Ireland, blissfully unaware of its superfood status, for many years, used more often as outwinter feed for dairy cattle than greens on our human plates. It is very good roasted with a little oil and salt as a virtuous early evening nibble. Add a little sugar for a caramel crunch.

For 6 to 8
5 minutes preparation
10 minutes cooking

3 large leaves of kale, stalks removed
2 tablespoons rapeseed oil
1 tablespoon Demerara sugar
1 teaspoon sea salt flakes

Pre-heat the oven to 180 °C.

Tear the kale into bite sized pieces and set them on some foil on a baking sheet.

Sprinkle with oil, salt and sugar and bake for about 10 minutes, keeping a very close eye on them. The turning point between "crispy" and "burned" is a very fine one.

Remove from the oven and let them cool for a while. Serve warm or cold.

SEA KALE

Sea Kale is an unusual and rare seaside plant, native to Ireland, that grows wild on shingly beaches but for centuries has been cultivated in Irish kitchen gardens. Its thick, blue-green leaves have a natural protective wax to allow them to survive the wind and salt, and when grown domestically, the plants are often covered to allow the leaves to develop so they can be more easily cooked. Sea kale has a short season but it is an excellent and tasty vegetable, cooked just like kale and cabbage.

Stephen Facciola in foragers' bible Cornucopia II says this: "The blanched leafstalks are eaten raw in salads, boiled, baked, braised or otherwise prepared as asparagus. When properly cooked they retain their firmness and have a very agreeable flavor, somewhat like that of hazelnuts, with a very slight bitterness. The leaves can be boiled until soft, minced, seasoned with garlic, and served as spinach."

CREAMED KALE WITH NUTMEG

In *Irish Traditional Food*, Theodora FitzGibbon tells us that kale is known as "Raggedy Jack" in Mayo and Donegal "on account of its serrated leaves", and that this way of cooking it — boiled or steamed and mixed with cream — was her father's favourite method. It is certainly a more forgiving dish than many of today's on-trend recipes using raw kale.

For 4
5 minutes preparation
30 minutes cooking

1 kg kale
75 g butter
2 tablespoons double cream
Nutmeg, salt and pepper to taste
100 ml vegetable stock

Cut the hard stems from the middle of the kale leaves and rinse well.

Bring a pot of water to the boil and cook the leaves in it for 25 minutes or so, until they are quite soft.

Drain them well.

Melt the butter in a shallow pan with the cream, a pinch of nutmeg, salt and pepper. Add the warm kale and the stock, and cook, stirring from time to time, for a few minutes until the sauce has reduced and the kale is tender. Add the cream and stir. Check the seasoning and serve nice and hot with pork, beef or game, or as a dish on its own with, perhaps, a poached egg on top and some good Irish cheddar grated over the lot.

A good addition, too, are mushrooms, beefing up the taste and texture. As the kale is cooking, fry the mushrooms (button, chanterelle, ceps, parasol or hedgehog) in butter with a finely chopped shallot until they are brown and soft. Add some double cream and mix into the tender kale in the other pan.

Browned butter is also terrific with kale, so instead of using cream, heat gently in a small saucepan around 50 g of unsalted butter until it turns brown and nutty. Fry some bacon pieces with onions or shallots in a pan next to it and mix them all with the kale once it has cooked in the stock. Serve with chopped parsley.

JUICING
ORANGES
€2

CLASS I

Roy Fox gourmet store, Donnybrook.

MASHED CARROTS AND PARSNIPS WITH A TON OF BUTTER, WHITE PEPPER AND COOLATTIN CHEDDAR

When I was a child, carrots and parsnips were an almost exotic accompaniment to the steak and kidney braised in thick gravy and baked pastry triangles with which they would usually be served.
I loved the sweetness, of course, the pungency of the parsnip, how the bright colours stayed separate, and the way they wouldn't soak up the butter quite as quickly as mashed potatoes did. Now meat is a rarity in my weekly cooking, and very often this dish will be a simple winter supper in its own right, jazzed up with good pepper and proper salted butter.

It was the Irish restaurant critic and wine writer, Tom Doorley, who introduced me to Tom Burgess' red-crusted, raw milk Coolattin cheddar from Wicklow, one summer Sunday afternoon in County Cork.
We had arrived rather late at Tom's jolly party, and the hefty slice on his generous dining room table was beginning to disappear fast. I'm very glad we got there in time.

It's a magnificent cheese, made only during the summer months when the cows are grazing clover — rich grass. Full flavoured and nutty, it works well grated over the warm, buttery, crushed carrots and parsnips.

For 4
5 minutes preparation
25 minutes cooking

500 g each carrots and parsnips, peeled and chopped into large chunks
AT LEAST 100 g good salted butter
Pepper
125 g Coolattin cheddar

Bring a pot of water to the boil and steam the pieces of carrots and parsnip over it for about 25 minutes until tender, but not too soft.

Set them into a bowl, cut about three quarters of the butter into them and let it melt through.Mash the vegetables by hand with a masher or a fork.

Season with pepper, dot the rest of the butter on top, grate the cheese over the warm vegetables and serve.

ROOT VEGETABLES GLAZED IN BUTTER AND TIPPERARY HONEY WITH SEA SPAGHETTI

Such a simple, easy way to cook root vegetables and make the most of their lovely colours. I would steer clear of beetroot or purple carrots here as colours seep into water and make everything murky. Carrots, parsnips and celeriac work best.

You can, of course, use a spiralizer or a mandolin in this dish, but I possess neither and my vegetable peeler does it all quite nicely, with the liquorice-lookalike sea spaghetti adding an interesting bite.

For 4
1 hour soaking in advance for the seaweed
10 minutes preparation
10 minutes cooking

2 carrots
2 parsnips or about ½ a celeriac
A handful of dried sea spaghetti
100 g butter
1 tablespoon runny Irish honey
Salt and pepper

Soak the dried sea spaghetti in water for an hour or so before starting the recipe. If you have fresh seaweed, rinse it thoroughly, simmer for about 10 minutes and drain.

Peel the vegetables then peel long ribbons from them, twisting them as you go.

Bring a saucepan of water to the boil and blanche the vegetables for about a minute. Heat the butter with the honey and a tablespoon of water in a heavy based pan until it is simmering.

Drain the veg and tip them into the pan. Simmer gently for five minutes or so, stirring from time to time, until the ribbons are tender and nicely coated with the reduced butter honey glaze. Add the sea spaghetti halfway through to warm it up.

Serve immediately seasoned with a little salt and back pepper.

CLASSIC APPLE AND BEETROOT RELISH

The only beetroot I knew in Ireland before arriving in France was the rather harshly pickled kind which puckered my lips and stained the boiled eggs on Sunday night salad plates. In the 1970s, I remember fondly the garish array of "salad jellies" my mother would make to go with cold leftover roast beef and ham — fresh cucumber with lime, shredded carrot with orange and (my favourite) pickled beetroot with blackcurrant or raspberry. I, for one, was never surprised when, years later, my French friends told tales of being traumatised by jelly as children on school exchanges.

Happily this sweet, earthy vegetable loves our Irish soil and is now enjoying a revival *sans le jelly*. Steam, boil or roast them and serve with cheese, beef or game.

The winter stored beet are best slow roasted in their skins, wrapped in foil or encased in a salt crust, in a low oven for about 2 hours. If you can push the skin from the beetroot with your fingers it's cooked. Young summer beetroot is best steamed or boiled. They will take about 30 minutes whole, about 15 cut into chunks.

Serve hot beetroot tossed in rapeseed oil with some good salt and pepper. It needs very little else.

This relish, with its pickled cucumber counterpart, can be found everywhere in Ireland, and with the apples and gentle spices, it is an altogether more palatable affair than your usual supermarket brands.

For 6 x 250 ml jars
15 minutes preparation
1 hour cooking

500 g fresh beetroot
1 kg cooking apples
250 g onions
300 g Demerara sugar
1 teaspoon salt
2 or 3 crushed peppercorns
3 or 4 crushed fennel seeds
750 ml red wine vinegar

Peel and chop the apples, onions and beetroot. Put them in a large pan with the sugar, pepper, fennel and vinegar. Give everything a good stir.

Bring to the boil, then reduce the heat and simmer for about one hour, stirring from time to time until the beetroot is tender.

Spoon into sterilized jars and seal. Leave them to cool. Keep the jars in the refrigerator and use them within a month or so.

BEETROOT POACHED IN LARD, STEAMED OR PICKLED, RAPESEED OIL, SEA SALT AND DILL

Here's a little suggestion for a pretty beetroot plate to make the most of the coloured varieties often on sale at good farmers' markets. The lard is fun, but use vegetable oil if you are reticent. Poaching in oil gives the beet a nice crunchy crust.

If you find the beetroot total look a little too austere, serve it with some thinly sliced Dunmanus cheese, or a fresh goats' cheese. Tender beet leaves would also be delicious with this, dressed as a salad.

For 6
30 minutes cooking
10 minutes plating

3 or 4 small multi-coloured beets
250 g lard
or 250 ml vegetable oil
a small jar of beetroot pickle
3 tablespoons good rapeseed oil
Sea salt flakes
Fresh dill

Peel the beets. Steam half of them over boiling water.

Poach the others in the oil or lard in a saucepan, taking care not to burn yourself or set the kitchen on fire! Keep an eye on the beets so they do not become too darkened. Remove from the pan with a slotted spoon and drain on some kitchen paper. Keep warm.

Slice the steamed and poached beets very thinly and set on warmed plates. Sprinkle with oil and salt and garnish with the pickled beetroot and dill.

SIMPLE MARINATED BEETROOT

1 small, raw beetroot
2 tablespoons rapeseed oil
1 tablespoon good Irish vinegar
½ teaspoon sugar
Fresh thyme, a pinch of salt and pepper

Mix the oil, vinegar and sugar together, season with salt and pepper. Peel and slice the beetroot then slice very thinly — with a mandoline if you have one.

Set the beetroot into the marinade, making sure it is completely covered. Cover the bowl with cling film and leave in the fridge overnight.

SCALLOP, PARSLEY, MUSHROOM, BEETROOT, BY STEVIE TOMAN

For 4
30 minutes preparation
45 minutes cooking

4 scallops
1 large crapaudine beetroot
1 cup of washed chanterelles (if you have trompettes these will also work — Stevie changes the dish according to what's available)
1 cauliflower
1 l milk
10 g butter
150 g picked flat-leaf parsley
50 g washed baby spinach leaf
400 ml blanching water
40 g butter (for emulsion)

Wash and steam beetroot until tender, allow to cool.

When cool, peel and thinly slice on mandolin lengthways to retain shape.

Wash and chop cauliflower and cover with milk in pot, season with salt and gently cook until soft pass, then through a sieve (keeping liquid). Purée until smooth, adding liquid if needed to obtain a smooth consistency, pass through sieve and check seasoning.

Blanch spinach and parsley in a pot of boiling water for 45 seconds, then refresh in ice water.
Squeeze dry and place into liquidiser with 400 ml of blanching water, then puree until it's a smooth, green liquid.

Pass through fine sieve and season with salt, add emulsion butter and gently heat. Set to the side but keep warm while you cook the scallop. Sauté scallop in a non-stick pan until golden and cooked (approx 2 minutes each side). Rest for 2 minutes.

In the meantime, foam the spinach and parsley liquid with a hand blender and spoon into hot bowl.
Add a spoonful of cauliflower purée.

Cut scallop in half and place in a hot bowl. Quickly sauté the mushrooms, season with salt and pepper, scatter over scallop. Garnish with warmed beetroot slice and sprinkle of fleur de sel.

(The pic has micro fennel as garnish, but you could use fennel shoots)

CREAM,
BUTTER,
CHEESE
AND BUTTERMILK

Triskel goat's milk cheese by Amia l'Eveque at Sheridans Cheesemongers, Galway.

BOILED CAKE

During my studies I spent a year as a teaching assistant in Antibes, on the Cote d'Azur. This cake, requiring only a saucepan and a cake tin to make, was perfect cooking for my tiny kitchenette and the gift I would always bring when I was invited over to friends to eat. Soon, the word got out. "Hi Trish. Come for dinner? Oh, and could you bring some of that *gâteau irlandais*?" I love its practicality, and the improbability of such simplistic technique (can one even call it baking?) turning out something so rich and good. A well known and equally simple version is the tea brack, where the dried fruit is steeped and softened in strong tea.

For 6 to 8
20 minutes preparation
1 hour cooling
45 to 50 minutes cooking

225 ml water
110 g salted butter
200 g soft brown sugar
150 g currants
150 g sultanas
2 teaspoons mixed spice
225 g self raising flour
1 beaten egg

Put the fruits, sugar, water and butter into a saucepan, bring to the boil and simmer for about 10 minutes. Leave to cool completely. Pre-heat the oven to 180 °C. Add the sieved flour, spices and beaten egg to the fruit mixture, stir thoroughly and pour into a medium greased and lined (or silicone) medium loaf tin. Bake for 45 to 50 minutes, checking the centre of the cake with a knife or a skewer towards the end. If the cake starts darkening too much while it bakes, protect the top with foil to prevent it burning. Leave to cool completely in the tin before turning out. Serve toasted and buttered. Thickly. With strong tea.

YOUNG BUCK OAT COOKIES

Young Buck raw milk blue cheese is the daring creation of 27-year-old entrepreneur cheesemaker Mike Thomson. Mike fell in love with cheese and cheesemaking while working at Belfast's renowned deli, Arcadia.
He trained with some of the UK's best artisan cheese producers before returning to his homeland to create Young Buck.
Cooking its Stilton-like, lemony creaminess into these buttery biscuits (tweaked from Master Dan Lepard's recipe) was a joy.

For 12 cookies
10 minutes preparation
4 hours chilling
20 minutes cooking

80 g porridge oats
200 g Young Buck cheese, rinds off, crumbled
100 g unsalted butter, softened
2 egg yolks
1 tablespoon cold water
150 g flour

Toast the oats in the pan or on a baking tray in the oven at 180 °C for about 10 minutes. Leave them to cool completely.

With electric beaters, or in a food processor, mix the cheese, butter, egg yolks and water until smooth. Add the cooled oats and the flour and mix in thoroughly. Roll the dough into a sausage of about 3 cm diameter. Wrap it snugly in cling film and chill in the fridge for at least 4 hours.

Pre-heat the oven to 160 °C. Take the dough sausage straight from the fridge and slice it into discs of about 1 cm. Place these on a baking sheet lined with paper or silicone and bake for 20 minutes or so, until the biscuits are golden around the edges. Take them out of the oven and serve warm – I dare you to resist! – or cold.

EASY OAT CAKES FOR CHEESE

Every Irish cooking repertoire should include these crunchy, wholesome biscuits, ready in no time and perfect with Irish cheese.

For 12 to 15 oatcakes
5 minutes preparation
20 minutes baking

450 g oatmeal
225 g plain flour
125 g butter, melted
5 tablespoons lukewarm water
1 teaspoon bicarbonate of soda
1 teaspoon salt

Pre-heat the oven to 190 °C. Sift the flour with the salt and bicarbonate of soda. Mix in the oatmeal, add the butter and the water and bring together into a soft dough. Roll the dough out into 3 mm thickness, and cut into 5 cm rounds with a cookie cutter. Place on a greased baking tray and bake for 20 minutes or so, until crisp and golden.

DAVID HURLEY

Gregans Castle is a magical place in an extraordinary part of Ireland. Loved by JR Tolkein and CS Lewis – who were surely inspired by the scenery? – it sits at the foot of Corkscrew Hill, with long views out over the peeled Burren landscape towards Ballyvaughan and the coast. A very special corner of the world indeed. DAVID HURLEY took over the kitchens after the departure of Mickael Viljanen to The Greenhouse in Dublin. With such a mentor, and a formative six years with Paul Flynn at the Tannery in Dungarvan, he was well prepared to manage the luxury hotel's kitchens.

Hurley describes his cooking as "classical French done lighter". Under Paul Flynn's influence, his flavours are full-on and gutsy, even if his presentation is very much 2015 fine dining, right down to the couture, three-tiered, afternoon tea served in the elegant drawing room, or on the lawns in summer.

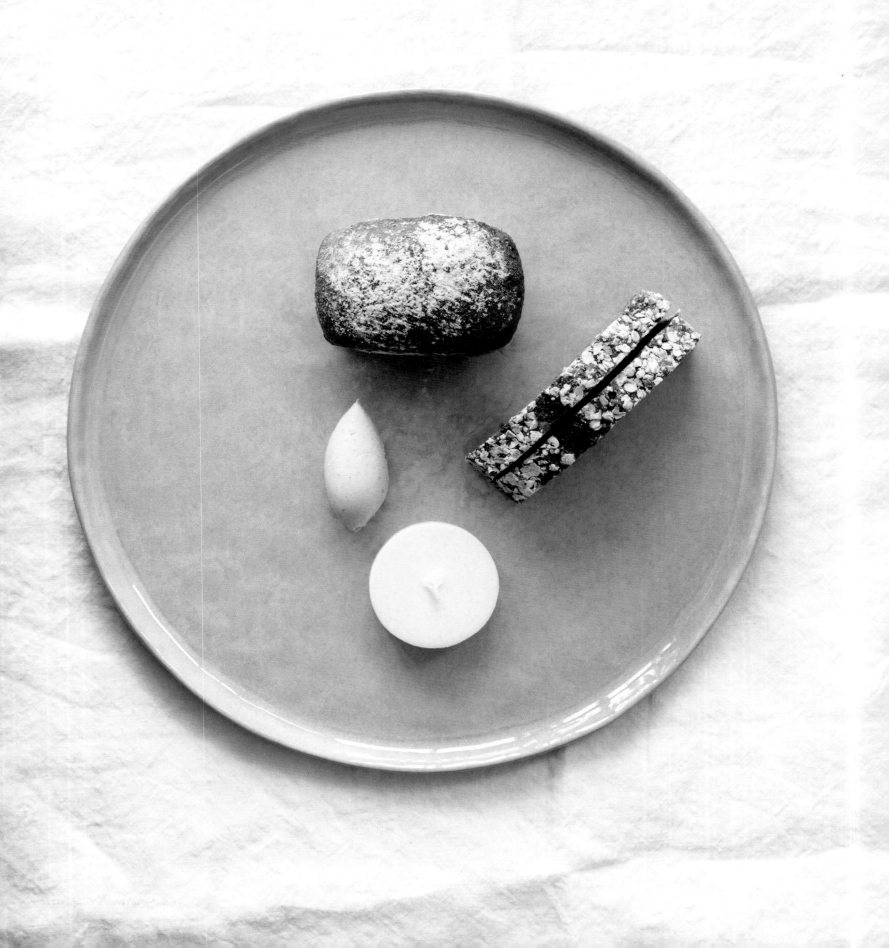

WHIPPED BUTTER, BY DAVID HURLEY AT GREGANS CASTLE

"Here at Gregans Castle hotel we like to use this butter as a way of 'preserving', if you like, the lovely, unmistakeable flavour of wild garlic, which usually has a short season (from March to April, depending on the weather). It grows in abundance a couple of fields away from us and, best of all, is free, thanks to Mother Nature! When the season is in full swing, we start to make the base butter, which we then freeze in small batches, allowing us to use it long after the season is finished. A handy staple in any freezer, it can be used to dress pasta, or finish a nice sauce. Any soft herbs can be used in place of the wild garlic."

For 8
3 hours preparation
10 minutes cooking

A handful of wild garlic leaves
227 g salted butter for the base
Salted butter for whipping

Wash the wild garlic leaves very well, drain and squeeze out excess water. Melt the butter. Roughly chop the wild garlic leaves and place in a food processor with the warm butter, then puree until as smooth as you prefer.

Pour the blended butter into an ice cube tray and freeze until set, then cover with cling film.

For the whipped butter, place the diced room temperature butter in a bowl.

Remove the butter base from the freezer (the more herbs you've managed to pack into this, the less you will need), melt gently and pour onto the diced butter. Whip with an electric mixer until light and fluffy. Serve with some good rustic bread.

BUTTER FOR HICKEY'S FAMOUS BARMBRACK

It is extremely easy to make your own butter. In fact, if you have ever curdled cream by whipping it for too long, you were halfway there already. All it takes is a whisk (electric unless you have superpowers) and some double cream and you will soon have added a hugely satisfying cooking skill to your list.

The barmbrack in the photo is from Hickey's bakery in Clonmel and is one of the best known and loved in Ireland. Moist and spicy, it is best served toasted with strong Irish tea. Barmbrack, like colcannon, is traditionally eaten at Halloween and can contain all sorts of hidden charms, coins and little jewels.

For about 175 g butter
40 minutes preparation

500 ml double cream at room temperature
½ teaspoon sea salt, flakes or fine (optional)

Pour the cream into a cold mixing bowl. Whip the cream until it is thick, then keep whipping. The cream will flatten, then split, with the buttermilk separating from the butterfat. You will end up with lots of tiny yellowish blobs in a whitish liquid.

Set a muslin cloth over a bowl and drain the liquid from the fat, twisting and squeezing the cloth to get as much moisture out as possible.

Keep the milk to make soda bread or scones. This is real buttermilk, and does not have the acidic twang you are used to. Do not waste it! It is also very good to drink.

Return the butter to the bowl and beat again for a further 30 seconds to 1 minute. Then drain it again. The more liquid you drain out, the less quickly the butter will go off. Lazy me tends to make a smaller amount and eat it quickly.

You can also work the butter in a bowl by hand, with butter pats and fresh water, changing it until it runs clear.

This is the stage at which you can flavour the butter, by whisking in the flavourings before setting it into a mould or forming shapes. Make sure you work quickly, with a bowl of ice water to cool the butter quickly after you have handled it. I like to keep things very simple, and make a roundish dome shape or press the butter into a dish or a mould for serving.

The Dark He

Co. Antrim..

VEDA TOASTED
WITH BUTTER
AND BONE MARROW

Veda is a very rare thing in these days of ultra-connected, web-delivered foodism. It's a loaf (of dark, sweet, soft malted bread, originating in Scotland) which is only available inside Northern Ireland. Only kindly friends and relatives can be counted on to relieve expats' nostalgia. And I speak from bitter experience, can you tell?

I suppose you could say it is Northern Ireland's Tarte Tatin, as it was first baked, the story goes, from damp, sprouted wheat, mistakenly taken for dry.

And there are still no official recipes for Veda. The few bakeries who sell it guard their secrets carefully, though there are a few honorable attempts to replicate the dense, fudgey feel and toasted malt taste. As with all of Ireland's breads, and many of its cakes (the boundary between the two being deliciously blurred), Veda is a perfect recipient for a thick layer of salted butter. Toasted, the first layer soaks quickly into its spongy texture, allowing an immediate second layer on the warm Veda of whatever you fancy – roasted bone marrow, Whiskey marmalade, Coleraine cheddar or, my favourite, more butter.

For 4
5 minutes preparation
15 minutes cooking

4 slices Veda bread
75 g butter, or more if you prefer/insist.
2 or 3 slices of bone with marrow
Sea salt

Pre-heat the oven to 180 °C.

Take the butter out of the fridge.

Put the bones in an ovenproof dish or on a baking sheet and roast for a good 10 minutes or so, until the marrow is bubbling slightly. Remove from the oven.

Just before serving, toast the Veda and spread it with butter.

Serve the bones with the slices of buttered toast, using little spoons to dig into the marrow and spread or set on the bread with a sprinkling of sea salt flakes.

BUTTER POTTED SCALLIONS WITH FENNEL

Not too many centuries ago, most small farms would have a cow, and milk, cream and butter were plentiful. The ancient Irish tradition of preserving food in butter has mostly died out now, although butter-preserved eggs are still available at the English Market in Cork. This recipe (made for eating, not keeping, so I haven't clarified the butter) is great with steamed or boiled root vegetables, and is a little nod to the old times.

For 6
3 minutes preparation
30 minutes cooking

300 g salted butter
2 scallions
A few grains of wild fennel

Melt the butter in a small saucepan and drop the scallions in.

Bring it to a gentle simmer and let the scallions poach with the fennel for 30 minutes or so until tender.

Pop the scallions into little pots or bowls and pour the butter over them.
Leave to cool before putting them in the fridge to chill.

PICKLED BUTTER

In the days of single cow farms, butter would be made each day from the cream of the milk and stored in brine or buttermilk.

In writer and broadcaster Florence Irwin's *The Cookin' Woman* (1949) she describes a method for "pickling" butter given to her by a lady in Warrenpoint, which "proved invaluable to literally thousands of people during the war years" and which Florence broadcast from Radio Eireann.

Freshly made butter (in half pound blocks wrapped in muslin, never from a newly calved cow's milk) was dropped into a pickle crock full of brine with a lid and a "well scoured stone to weight it". Week by week, the butter was thus preserved, kept emerged in the brine with the stone in the dairy or airy larder.

The butter could be used once the muslin was removed and the salt water washed away. Florence writes, "If the dairy cleanliness had been observed" and the butter was "sweet and fresh" when it entered the pickle crock, it could keep for nine to twelve months.

GOOD THINGS CAFE DURRUS CHEESE, SEA BEET AND NUTMEG PIZZA

This is chef and owner Carmel Somers' much loved recipe.

For 4 (2 large pizzas)
20 minutes preparation
1 hour resting
10 minutes cooking

For 1 pizza dough — if you manage to roll the dough very thin you will have extra for another day
500 g white bread flour and a little more for kneading
1 x 7 g sachet instant dried yeast
10 g salt
350 ml tap water

For the garnish
4-5 large handfuls of roughly chopped sea beet, stalks removed
Salt, pepper and lots of freshly grated nutmeg
12 thin slices Durrus cheese (about 200 g) with rind removed
Olive oil
Handful of fine brown flour for rolling

Make the pizza dough. Take your largest, widest mixing bowl and tip in the flour, yeast, salt and almost all of the water, and mix to a sticky dough. Keep mixing until the dough becomes less sticky, then add a little more flour until you have a dough that is soft and springy.

Generously flour a large, flat work surface and scoop the dough out on to it. Work the dough with your hands. Keep this up for ten minutes. If you find this exhausting then you are pushing too hard. Place the ball of dough back in the bowl, cover it with a clean tea towel and put it somewhere warm, but not hot, for an hour or so. OR if you are planning ahead, put in a sealed container and store in the fridge until needed.

Heat oven to hottest and heat two flat-sided baking trays. This is essential for a crispy base.

Divide the pizza dough in half and roll each piece very thinly using the fine flour to dust the worktop.

Place on the hot baking tray and top with the sea beet. Season with salt, pepper and grated nutmeg.

Arrange the slices of cheese on top.

Drizzle with olive oil and bake in the hot oven for 8 – 10 minutes until the base is golden and crispy and the cheese has melted.

Notes
Instead of sea beet you can use Swiss chard, beetroot tops or spinach.
If you cannot get Durrus cheese, use a strong semi-soft cheese, preferably unpasteurised as the flavour is better for cooking.

IRISH BROSE WITH FRUIT CORDIALS

Atholl Brose is a well known Scottish dish, but it is thought that Brose (from "broth" meaning goodness – as in "Pat's the broth of a good fellow himself.") originated in Ireland. Here, I've used it to show off some of the fine fruit cordials you find these days in Ireland made from a host of garden or foraged fruit and berries.

For 4
1 hour soaking
5 minutes preparation

4 tablespoons rolled oats
300 ml double cream
1 tablespoon runny Irish honey
2 tablespoons Irish whiskey
Drizzle of elderflower, blackcurrant, strawberry, ginger cordial

Soak the oats in boiling water for an hour. Drain them, pressing them into a sieve to remove as much water as possible.

Beat the cream until stiff, then fold in the whiskey and honey. Stir in the oats and serve with fresh fruit, drizzled with cordial.

MARK DIACONO'S ELDERFLOWER CORDIAL

Affable, funny and super knowledgeable writer and gardener Mark Diacono makes me believe I could grow and cook anything in my fantasy future garden.
"If you are new to or hesitant about foraging, let elder be the gateway into a world of free, delicious food." He says, soothingly. Here's his recipe for elderflower cordial, with thankfully no need for scary citric acid from the chemist's.

About 25 elderflower heads
Pared zest of 4 unwaxed lemons, plus the juice
900 g sugar

Shake the flowers to dislodge any insects, but don't bother washing them. Strip the flowers from the stems with a fork and place in a bowl together with the lemon zest. Pour 1,5 litres of water over, cover and leave overnight.

Strain through muslin into a saucepan. Add the sugar and lemon juice, warm and stir to dissolve the sugar, then simmer for a couple of minutes. Pour into sterilised bottles and seal. Dilute to taste when drinking, and keep in the fridge once opened.

AUNTIE BEATTIE'S PINEAPPLE DELIGHT

In my family, we call this pudding "Beattie's Thing". Beattie is my Aunt — 93 and still as fresh as a daisy. It has all the vital elements of a Northern Irish 1970s dinner party dessert — whipped cream, crushed digestive biscuits, tinned fruit and crumbled Flake chocolate on top. It takes 30 minutes to assemble, and even though it has never quite left my repertoire, I feel it's due, if not a full-on homage, at least a little limelight. There are many spin-offs — from cousins, girlfriends and daughters-in-law — but this is the version which most satisfies my nostalgia and memories of good family times in Belfast. I still find it hilarious how excitingly subversive the use of crushed biscuits in desserts seemed to the French in my first cookbook back in 1999. (I've added below my go-to semi-scandalous, no-bake "cheesecake" pud of those days, made with packets of biscuits AND jelly).

I doubt the Irish taste for the cream and good old buttery biscuit combo will ever change, though here I've left the Flake out as Cadbury's chocolate has been so tampered with I now find it inedible. And that's saying something. Track down a decent bar of milk chocolate to grate if you absolutely want to use it.

For 8 to 10
30 minutes preparation
2 hours resting

350 g ginger nut biscuits (one and a half packets)
50 g slightly salted butter
400 g tinned, crushed pineapple
350 ml double or whipping cream
1 tablespoon icing sugar

Crush the biscuits into not-too-fine crumbs. Melt the butter and mix it into the biscuit crumbs. Press the crumbs into a 22 cm springform tin and pop into the fridge to harden.

Drain the juice from the pineapple and spread over the biscuit base. Whip up the cream, add the icing sugar, mix and top the pineapple, smoothing it out.

Leave it in the fridge for an hour or so before removing from the tin and serving with Flake on top (or not).

MY CHEATS' LEMON CHEESECAKE

The procedure is the same as the Pineapple Delight. Start with the biscuit base of digestive biscuits and let it cool. Melt a lemon jelly in the heated juice of two lemons, add the lemon grated zest, let it all cool slightly. Whisk the cream with 300 g of cream cheese (or even "real" mild and creamy goats' cheese!) until firm, mix the lemon liquid well through it all and leave to set for a couple of hours in the fridge. Decorate with thin lemon slivers.

GOODY

There are versions of this, perhaps the ultimate cheap and cheerful comfort food, in many parts of the world. In Ireland, the most common is made with white bread (crusts on!) sugar, a pinch of cinnamon and hot milk.

For 1
5 to 10 minutes preparation

2 slices white pan bread
2 teaspoons brown sugar
Pinch of cinnamon
150 ml or so hot milk

Tear the bread into pieces and place in a saucepan. Pour the hot milk over, sprinkle with sugar and let it soak into the bread for a minute before bringing to the boil.

Let it cool, sprinkle with a pinch of cinnamon and a little more sugar before serving and eating with a spoon.

Some versions have the soaked bread browned in the oven before serving. Some layer the bread, soak it and cook in the oven without boiling first. But you get the gist.

FOOD IN HARD TIMES

In ancient Ireland, well before potatoes became the staple crop, the peasant population lived mostly on grains and milk. A common drink amongst the very poor was known as "Bull's milk". It was made of oats fermented in water and tasted like diluted vinegar.

"Beestings" is the first milk drawn from a cow after calving. In some parts of Ireland it was not used for human consumption at all — presumably a better deal for the baby calf — but in others (Donegal, Tyrone, Antrim) it was highly rated. Thick and yellow, thanks to the rich colostrum content, it was unsuitable for butter making but much prized for making pancakes and curd cheese.

Their milk was not the only thing Irish native cattle sacrificed. It's said that "a Kerry cow knows when it's Sunday", for on Sundays, in the very worst of times and in the most remote parts of Ireland, the only sustenance was cows' blood, drawn from them, as it was from camels in Africa when food and water ran out.

"Stirabout" was another traditional name given to porridge. Made with oats, barley or wheat boiled with cow's or sheep's milk, it was generally eaten with honey, butter or fresh milk. The very poor made it with buttermilk or water.

BALLYWALTER PARK, BALLYWALTER, CO. DOWN

Home to Lord and Lady Dunleath, Ballywalter Park is first and foremost a lively, thriving family residence. Brian Mulholland has remained true to the entrepreneurial spirit of his ancestors, who became the biggest cotton and linen manufacturers in the world during the late 19th century, as well as figuring amongst Northern Ireland's most distinguished politicians and public servants. He has not only maintained this exquisite palazzo style house, one of only three Charles Lanyon designed houses in Northern Ireland, but through various activities, including luxury incentive tours and its use as a film location for period dramas, has restored and improved Ballywalter to an extent that it is even more beautiful and cherished today than it has ever been.

Brian and his wife, Danish food historian Vibse Dunleath, have restored and developed the gardens and park immeasurably, with the beautiful Victorian glasshouses in the walled garden growing marvellous Hamburg grapes and fat peaches and apricots alongside sweet strawberries, many varieties of fancy kale, tomatoes, salad leaves and herbs.

Vibse writes regularly about her work (and cooking!) in the house and gardens in her blog on Ballywalter's website, bringing this special place even more to life. One day perhaps, you will be lucky enough to find yourself in the spectacular conservatory, drinking tea and trying one of Vibse's famous Eccles cakes with a nibble of Young Buck blue cheese!

Such is the wealth of choice and quality of what is grown here, that Vibse and Brian make regular trips with overflowing baskets to OX restaurant in Belfast, where Stevie Toman works his magic with Ballywalter's produce. The estate's main activity today is a state of the art dairy farm with a herd of 420 pedigree Holstein-Friesians. Recently, Vibse has been experimenting with the production of rose veal from bull calves, which Stevie likes to serve raw with smoked potato on the ever evolving OX menu.

Lord and Lady Dunleath at the gates of their walled garden at Ballywalter House.

Ballywalter House, Vibse and Brian Dunleath and produce from the walled garden.

BARLEY BAKED WITH CREAM, CAULIFLOWER, DURRUS CHEESE AND O'NEILL'S STREAKY BACON

A sort of de-potatoed tartiflette, the barley and cauliflower lighten up the dish and give texture where once there was stodginess. I have also suggested adding a little thyme and lemon to make it more interesting, but there's nothing stopping you sticking with spuds and onions under the cheese, like a real tartiflette, if you so desire – this is one dish where the straight substituting of Irish for French ingredients is definitely a good move. In fact, with Durrus cheese, our home grown potatoes and bacon, it's possibly even an improvement on the original.

For 4
20 minutes preparation
5 minutes cooking

250 g pearl barley
100 g or so fresh cauliflower florets (frozen at a pinch)
4 to 8 rashers of good streaky smoked bacon
20 g butter
150 ml double cream
Salt and pepper
Thyme, grated lemon zest (optional)
One small Durrus cheese (300 g)

Pre-heat the oven (or grill) to 180 °C.

Bring a pan of lightly salted water to the boil and cook the barley until it's tender – around 20 min. In another pan, do the same and cook the cauliflower for about 15 minutes, until it is soft enough to put a knife through.

Meanwhile, fry the bacon rashers in a little butter until they are nice and golden, but not too crispy as they still have some time to do in the oven. Keep them warm.

Drain the barley and cauliflower, then mix them together in a bowl with the cream, breaking up the cauliflower and spreading it through the barley. Season with salt and pepper and add the thyme and lemon zest if you are using them.

Put the barley and cauliflower into a medium gratin dish (or any medium-sized, shallow ovenproof dish with sides).

Slice the Durrus and lay it over the top, alternating with slices of bacon.

Put the dish under the grill or in the oven and heat for about 5 minutes, until the cheese is slightly golden and the cream is bubbling under it.

Remove from the oven and leave to cool slightly before serving with a crisp salad (or not).

DUNMANUS FRITTERS WITH SALAD LEAVES AND WARM POACHED PEAR

This recipe, by Dominique Carucci of Arundels in Ahakista, comes with the seal of approval of Jeffa Gill herself, maker of wonderful West Cork Dunmanus and Durrus cheeses.

For 4
25 minutes preparation
20 minutes cooking

2 pears
100 g sugar
1 vanilla pod, split down the middle
Juice of a lemon
200 g Dunamanus cheese
50 g butter
1 egg
100 ml milk
3 or 4 tablespoons flour
Salt and pepper
4 handfuls fresh salad leaves
2 tablespoons rapeseed oil
1 tablespoon cider vinegar

Bring 250 ml of water to the boil with the sugar and the vanilla pod and simmer for 5 minutes or so to reduce to a syrup.

Peel the pears, core and quarter them and poach in the syrup until tender – about 15 minutes. Add the lemon juice to the syrup and leave the pears to cool.

Prepare individual plates with the pears and the salad leaves tossed in the oil and vinegar with a little salt and pepper.

Cut the Dunmanus into triangles, removing the crust.

Spread the flour onto a flat plate and season very lightly with a little salt.

Put some kitchen paper on another in preparation for draining the excess butter from the cooked fritters.

Beat the egg with the milk in a bowl. Heat the butter in a heavy frying pan until it is bubbling.

Dip the first piece of cheese into the eggy milk, let it drip slightly before setting it onto the flour and turning it over, so the flour clings to the surface.

Fry the cheese fritter in the butter, turning until golden on all sides. Remove from the pan and drain on some kitchen paper.

Repeat until you've used up all the cheese pieces. Serve immediately with the salad and pears.

DEREK CREAGH

Donal Doherty persuaded fellow Donegal man DEREK CREAGH to come home from where he was working in England, with wife and children, and take on not only the kitchens at Donal's family restaurant Harry's in Bridgend Donegal, but also his "Made in Inishowen" philosophy of local sourcing of sustainable ingredients.

Derek also designed the menu for the wildly successful Harry's Shack right on Portstewart Strand on Nothern Ireland's Causeway Coast, bringing some of the favourites from the original restaurant eastwards to Portstewart.

His time spent in big kitchens, like Heston Blumenthal's Fat Duck, brings Harry's and Harry's Shack a serious boost. And, since August 2014, the sudden expansion has been carried off brilliantly, with many awards and rave reviews from Ireland and beyond.

BABY WHITE TURNIP SOUP, BY DEREK CREAGH, HARRY'S BRIDGEND

For 4
5 minutes preparation
20 minutes cooking

1 kg baby white turnip flesh
250 g butter
1 large potato, peeled and finely sliced
1 cooking apple, finely sliced
3 onions, finely sliced
1 bottle of Stonewell cider
400 ml milk
Rosemary and thyme
600 ml water/stock

Melt the butter in a large saucepan and sweat the onion, white turnip, apple and potato for approximately 10 minutes.

Pour in cider, stir and reduce until the alcohol has reduced, but not too much as you want to retain the cider's acidity.

In a separate pan, heat the milk with the rosemary and thyme and leave to infuse.

When the onions are translucent, add the herb infused milk.

Bring to the boil and simmer for a further 10 minutes.

Remove from heat, liquidise and pass through a fine strainer.

Season with salt and pepper.

View towards the coast near Cleggan, Connemara.

BUTTERMILK SCONES

As loved and as ubiquitous as soda bread around Ireland, scones are a handy thing to learn to make well, and a mini-meal unto themselves at 4 o'clock.

Once you get the hang of them, you can have them ready to serve in under 30 minutes and, really, they are at their very best just out of the oven. The egg in this recipe adds a little touch of golden richness I like, and the boost of bicarb to the self-raising flour will make your scones high and fluffy. The trick is not to handle the dough too much. Just like with the soda bread recipes on page 251, it needs shaping ('tidying up' as Darina Allen would say) rather than rolling out, and you must not be afraid of leaving it quite loose and wet. Some home bakers swear by grating the butter, frozen, into the dry ingredients. And certainly that is a handy thing to know if you've stored some in the freezer and forgotten to defrost it in time for tea. Serve the scones warm with strong tea, butter and any sort of sweet preserve.

For 10 scones
10 minutes preparation
20 minutes cooking

500 g self raising flour
50 g raisins or sultanas
1 teaspoon baking powder
1 teaspoon bicarbonate of soda
100 g salted butter, cold, cut into cubes
1 egg, beaten
200 ml buttermilk

Pre-heat the oven to 220 °C.

Line a baking sheet with paper.

With a light hand, sift the flour, raisins baking powder and bicarbonate of soda into a large bowl.
Beat the egg into the buttermilk.
Rub the butter in with your fingers until the mixture resembles breadcrumbs, then mix in the egg and the buttermilk.
Knead it quickly and lightly, making a soft, quite wet dough. Add a little flour to your hands if the dough is too sticky. Roll it out to about 2 cm height and cut out circles with a fluted cutter.

Set the scones onto the baking sheet, brush with a little of the eggy milk and bake for 15 to 20 minutes, until they are well risen and golden on top.

Remove from the oven and let them cool slightly. Serve hot, warm or cold.

CUCUMBER HERBS, GOATS CURD AND RAPESEED OIL

These light little niblets will leave your guests' tastebuds primed and appetites intact for what comes next. They behave reasonably well when prepared in advance and left in the fridge. Although it's perhaps best to wait for the last minute before doing the drizzling of the rapeseed oil.

For 6 to 8
25 minutes preparation

6 slices soda bread
50 g softened, salted butter
1 cucumber, peeled, sliced thinly
A handful of capers
A lemon
Dill, buckshorn plantain, samphire, oyster leaves for garnishing
Goats curd or cheese
Salt and pepper

Slice the bread thinly, tear into bite sized pieces and lightly butter it.

Lay two slices of cucumber on each piece of bread, then top with oyster leaf, dill and lemon pulp on one half, and goats cheese, capers and buckshorn plantain or dill on the other half. Season with a little salt and pepper, and drizzle with rapeseed oil just before serving.

TOMATO AND CUCUMBER SALAD WITH YOGHURT, CUCUMBER RELISH, MINT AND RAPESEED OIL

Irish summer salads of my childhood always seemed so lacklustre compared to those I grew to know and love in France. A few lettuce leaves, some tomato and cucumber, perhaps a little coleslaw as an afterthought was about your lot.

How things have changed! Here's a pretty, tasty way of putting our simple summer vegetables centre stage and letting them sing. And don't forget Nora Ephron's vital life rules: never keep your tomatoes in the fridge.

For 4
10 minutes preparation

2 or 3 large beefsteak tomatoes
8 or 10 cherry tomatoes
½ to ⅔ of a cucumber
250 g set yoghurt (or goats cheese or curd, or cottage cheese)
A small handful of fresh mint leaves
4 tablespoons cucumber relish
Rapeseed oil for garnish
Salt and pepper

Slice the cucumber and tomato thinly.

Dice the cherry tomatoes and crush them slightly with a fork.

Dress the plates by setting the tomato and cucumber slices down first, then dotting the yoghurt, cherry tomato pulp and relish here and there.

Garnish with mint leaves, season with salt, pepper and rapeseed oil.

FISH,
SEAFOOD,
SEAWEED

Balintoy harbour, Co. Antrim.

HEDERMAN'S GRAVLAX WITH LEMON BUTTER ON SODA BREAD

I first tasted this, balanced on the knife Frank Hederman had used to slice it, in its thickness, not making slivers along its length, at Midleton farmers' market in Cork. It is divine, delicate and firm, a million miles away from the more aggressively flavoured Scandi versions I was used to in France.

The picture is a serving suggestion, not a recipe. Sometimes it is best to leave the artistry to the artists and as I would never have the cheek to ask Frank for the secrets of his family's trade, I have included an easy one using Blackwater gin, made not a million miles from Hederman's smokery.
To serve either, all you do is grate a little untreated lemon zest into some good unsalted butter.
Mix and spread on good soda bread.

BLACKWATER GIN-CURED GRAVLAX

Ireland's craft gins are having a moment, and the excellent Blackwater gin from Waterford is a perfect example of how dying skills and traditions are being rekindled.

For 6 to 8
10 minutes preparation
48 hours curing

4 tablespoons coarse sea salt
4 tablespoons table sugar
2 tablespoons dill, chopped
3 or 4 juniper berries, crushed
2 tablespoons black peppercorns, crushed
3 tablespoons Blackwater gin
The grated zest of 2 lemons
A salmon filet of around 800g, with skin left on

Mix all the ingredients apart from the salmon together. Sprinkle the gin in last and stir quickly.

Place a wide layer of plastic film on a baking tray and spread half the cure mix onto it.

Place the salmon filet, with the skin side down, on the mix and spoon the rest over the top. Cover it evenly, pressing the mix into the flesh of the salmon.

Wrap the entire bundle tightly in more cling film and weigh it down with another baking tray or a chopping board, with a weight set on it. Put the whole lot in the fridge for 48 hours, turning the fish bundle every 12 hours.

After the two days, take the fish out of the cling film and rinse the cure off the surface, under cold running water. Dry the fish all over with kitchen paper or a tea towel.

To serve, slice the gravlax thinly along its side, or in more chunky, vertical cuts as Frank Hederman likes to do.

A MAGICAL CARRAGEEN REMEDY

One night in Ballydehob, West Cork, food writer Joe MacNamee made me a carrageen remedy to tackle my bad cold and cough. He made it with whiskey, and I could feel the delicious concoction doing good with every sip. The next day my cough was gone.

Here's Joe's note to me when, naturally, I asked him for this miraculous recipe.

Hi Trish,

This is just the latest version of a recipe I first came up with about 15 years ago. Like all recipes, I am constantly tinkering, never able to leave well enough alone, even when I achieve perfection in the eyes of others. But the constituent ingredients (Foley's Famous Five – carrageen, cinnamon, cloves, honey, apple juice) remain the same, it is just the technique that has altered.

What has never changed is the primary ingredient, the heart of the recipe, carrageen. Like so many of us living on the wettest rock in the Atlantic, I am a "martyr to the chest", guaranteed two or three nasty chest infections a year and the antibiotics to go with them, so became curious about the properties of this "weed of the sea" when I read that it had formerly been a traditional Irish cure for bronchial complaints. It appears its purported benefits are not just old wives tales but have some basis in sound science, and at one stage, carrageen was in phase III trials as a microbiocide for treating AIDS. Neither will you fail to notice the ginger as it "warms" your chest almost immediately after consumption – it is a natural vasodilator and improves circulation.

The end result is certainly very soothing and, personally, I will vouch for its efficaciousness – I think I have taken two or three antibiotics at most in the decade and a half since I first began using this concoction – and the addition of brandy makes for a very fine drink altogether, a variation of a hot toddy; so good, in fact, that I have been known to drink it as a preventative, before any illness at all makes itself known!

For 2 or 3 doses
20 minutes preparation
40 minutes cooking

1 fist-sized ball of dried Carrageen, about the size of a tennis ball
3 cubic centimetres fresh root ginger, scrubbed, not peeled, sliced as thin as possible
5-6 cm cinnamon stick
5 or 6 whole cloves

To serve
1 litre pressed apple juice (not from concentrate, the fresher, the better)
Honey (ideally: local, non-blended, non-pasteurised, cold filtered)
And if gravely, gravely ill or, worse still, struck down by man-flu, brandy

Place ginger, cinnamon and cloves in a saucepan with 2 litres cold water, bring to the boil and then allow to simmer for at least 20 min (the longer you allow it to simmer, the more you will generate ginger "heat")

Leaving the pot still simmering, rinse the carrageen to remove any impurities and then place in bowl of cold water (about 5 litres) for 10 minutes to reconstitute. It may even begin to extrude its natural jelly after the 10 minutes, but either way, add to the still simmering "spice water", bring back to the boil and then let it simmer for 20 minutes at most. You may even stop it earlier if you notice the mix has passed the "jelly" stage and the carrageen itself is starting to break down.

Strain the liquid, add the apple juice and store in the fridge. Warm to serve as required, stirring in at least 1 tablespoon of honey and brandy if you are beyond all hope or simply need a metaphorical pat on the head.

SEARED SALMON IN VEGETABLE, FENNEL AND KOMBU BROTH

This is a beautifully versatile and practical, two-tiered dish. Easy enough for a quick weekday tea, it also works well as a prep-ahead supper for guests. The kombu flakes might give it a slight frog-pond look, but they add a lovely taste and slightly chewy texture to the soft veg and flaky fish.

For 4
10 minutes preparation
30 minutes cooking

1 medium carrot
1 medium parsnip
1 stick of celery
2 small potatoes
1 small onion
A chunk of smoky bacon or 3 or 4 lardons
A small piece of lemon zest
Salt and pepper
30 g butter
1 tablespoon vegetable oil
Fennel seeds, just a pinch.
1 litre good vegetable stock or water
400 g salmon fillets, preferably with their skin on
1 tablespoon dried Kombu flakes

Peel and chop the vegetables into roughly 2 cm chunks. In a wide, heavy bottomed saucepan, heat the butter and oil and sweat the vegetables with the fennel seeds and bacon together for 4 or 5 minutes, until the vegetables start to soften. Pour in the stock or water, stir, season lightly with salt and pepper and bring to the boil.

Reduce the heat and let the vegetables cook for about 20 minutes, until they are soft but still holding their shape nicely. At this stage, you could taste the cooking liquid and, if it needs a little boost, drain it off the veg and reduce by boiling for a minute or two before putting the vegetables back.

Add the Kombu and lemon zest and stir through the vegetable broth. Taste and season again with salt and pepper if needed.

Heat a griddle pan or a non stick pan. Cut the salmon into two-bite pieces and fry them, skin side down for a minute or two, seasoning and turning once or twice until they are nicely crispy on the skin side and still pearly inside.

Ladle the vegetables and broth into wide bowls, top with the salmon pieces and serve with some good toasted bread, a squeeze of lemon and perhaps a condiment like Wildfood's excellent Haw Sauce.

SALLY BARNES SMOKED TUNA MASH

"The people were nearly all men, dressed solemnly and hideously in their Sunday clothes; most of them had come straight from Mass without any dinner, true to that Irish instinct that places its fun before its food." From *Some Experiences of an Irish R.M.* by Somerville and Ross.

Woodcock smokery is in the pretty Cork village of Castletownshend near Skibbereen in County Cork. The main street, flanked with colourful terraced houses and the odd pub or small shop, dips steeply to the edge of the harbour, overlooked by the handsome church and 17th century castle built by Richard Townsend. It's a sleepy, romantic place, home to writer Edith Anna Somerville, co author of the Irish R.M. series of humorous novels on Irish life in the early 1900s. It's here that Sally Barnes smokes her wild fish, using only a time-honoured and traditional methodology, without adding any colourings or artificial preserves.

Wild salmon is in short supply in Ireland, but instead of turning to farmed stocks, Sally has preferred to diversify the fish she uses, including line-caught Irish tuna. Here I have included it in the most simple of Irish dishes: buttered potato mash. Add a drop of lemon juice perhaps, but not much else is needed.

For 2
10 minutes preparation
20 minutes cooking

2 or 3 good sized floury potatoes
50 ml warm milk
75 g butter
Salt and pepper
200 g Woodstock smoked tuna
Lemon juice

Peel and boil the potatoes for about 20 minutes until they are soft.

Mash them with the warm milk and add half the butter. Season with a little salt and pepper and a squeeze of lemon.

Flake the tuna through the hot potato mash, add the rest of the butter to melt on top and serve immediately.

HARRY'S SHACK, PORTSTEWART, CO. LONDONDERRY

When the National Trust approached Donal Doherty to take over their former lifeguard's hut, right at the entrance to spectacular and hugely popular Portstewart Strand, he knew he could not refuse. Donal had already completely transformed his family's restaurant, Harry's, in Donegal, only minutes from the centre of Derry, by sourcing only local ingredients from Inishowen for the menu and, a few years later, by hiring one of the best chefs in the industry, Derek Creagh.

With the help of the Trust, using trailblazing interior designers and architects Oscar and Oscar, Donal transformed the dull wooden shack into a modern, cosy dining space and bar, with a wood burning stove and fabulous bay windows allowing views of the beach, whilst keeping the elements out.

The food was soon getting rave reviews from all over Ireland and the UK. The towering burgers, unbelievably good fish and chips and gorgeous baking and desserts are going down a treat, and now the Shack is packed out all year round.

It's an important success story, not only about revitalizing a rather tired old seaside town, but also how possible it is to buy, cook and serve local ingredients, keeping business and strengthening ties within the community.

Manager Donal Doherty outside Harry's Shack.

MUSSELS IN CIDER WITH APPLES

To Northern Ireland chef Danny Millar, of Balloo House in County Down, for the idea of this dish, wolfed down (well, as fast as you can go with mussels) one summer evening in Danny's beautiful 400 year old pub after I had forgotten to eat lunch.

Off Loughros Point in Donegal, through boggy land where you'd quickly leave a boot, if not a leg, in the black mud if you didn't know your way, my friends have a secret mussel picking spot. The shells are clustered thickly, sitting low on the rocks, and the seals look on as you pick, intrigued by the invasion of strange, crouched humans and their buckets. Loughros mussels are meaty and enormous, covered in barnacles, full of silt, requiring a good spin in a concrete mixer to make them clean and smooth enough for the pot.

For 2
10 minutes preparation
5 minutes cooking

2 shallots, finely chopped
50 g butter
200 ml Irish cider — Stonewell is excellent
1 kg mussels, debearded and scrubbed
1 crisp apple
1 tablespoon chopped fresh parsley
A couple of tablespoons of double cream (optional)

Discard any mussels which stay open after the scrubbing.

In a large, deep pot, melt the butter and sweat the shallots with the parsley. Pour in the cider, stir and bring to the boil.

Add the mussels to the pot, put the lid on and leave them to steam.

Give the pot a good shake halfway through to move the mussels around and make sure they all get a blast of heat and cidery steam.

Once they are all open (discard any mussels which have not opened), take the pot off the heat and add the cream to the cooking juice if you are using it.

Serve in soup dishes with thinly sliced apple as garnish and good bread to do the mopping up.

CRAB TOES
IN WILD GARLIC
AND LEMON BUTTER

An increasingly common dish on many Irish pub menus, they are a finger-licking delight served simply in wild garlic and lemon butter with plenty of bread to soak up whatever gets left on the plate.

In Ireland, the claws are half shelled, making them handy to pick up and suck out their sweet flesh from the tips and around the cartilage. It's a hands-on feast, there is really no other way of doing it. Knives and forks are so inefficient you will look slightly ridiculous trying to use them.

But this tasty convenience hides a rather unpalatable truth – mostly the claws are harvested at sea, with the rest of the crab, still alive, thrown back into the water. For some, their claws will grow back, but most die. Apparently this practice is still considered sustainable. So now you know.

For 4
5 minutes preparation
10 minutes cooking

2 dozen crab toes
150 g salted butter
Grated zest of ½ lemon
2 leaves wild garlic
White pepper to taste
A good slice of sourdough bread, made into breadcrumbs

Pre-heat the oven to 180 °C.

Whizz the butter, lemon zest, wild garlic and pepper in a mini blender.

Place the claws in a gratin dish and dot the butter over them.
Sprinkle with breadcrumbs and bake for about 10 minutes, until the crumbs are golden and the butter bubbling.

Leave to cool slightly to save your fingers then serve with lots of good fluffy bread, fingerbowls and napkins.

BURNT SCALLOPS WITH TOMATO WATER AND OYSTER LEAVES

I know foodie people are always declaring dishes their "favourite" or "very favourite" or even "ABSOLUTE favourite", but I think that of all the recipes in the book, this is the one I prefer.

It is ridiculously easy to make, so very good for you, and encapsulates the mobility of good ingredients and new ideas in food from one country, or one cook, to another. Without going all Noma-in-Japan on you, let's say that the inspiration for what turned out to be a very Irish dish came from France. Firstly from a gorgeous dish tasted on Clown Bar's sunny terrasse in Paris, of oysters in tomato water, then from a Twitter snap of "burnt" (the lastest resto fad as we go to print) scallops at L'Arpege, Paris.

My composite version uses the visual beauty, flavour and texture balance of those two muses and stamps a huge "Ireland" on them thanks to our exciting produce.

You can forage for magical really-do-taste-like-oysters oyster leaves, I'm told, but the specialized restaurant suppliers sell them neatly packaged and they keep quite well. They are well worth the effort or the expense, believe me.

For 4
45 minutes preparation
2 minutes cooking

1 kg ripe tomatoes, chopped
A touch of rapeseed oil
½ teaspoon salt
Juice of ½ lemon
Oyster leaves
12 fresh scallops. Hand dived if possible. Definitely Irish. Room temperature.
Salt and pepper

Put the tomatoes in a fine sieve with the salt. Mix gently from time to time and let the juice collect until you have about 200 ml. Divide the water between 4 dishes, season with a little lemon juice and salt and pepper if needed. You can use the tomato pulp and seeds for a home made tomato sauce.

Use a blow torch if you have one (otherwise heat your grill until it's very hot) to char the surface of the scallops until they blacken.

Set them into the water, top with the oyster leaves, drizzle with a little rapeseed oil and serve immediately.

The Burren coastal road near Fanore, Co. Clare.

PAN ROASTED COD WITH ARTICHOKES, BY DAVID HURLEY AT GREGANS CASTLE

"For this dish, we pan roast a fillet of cod which has been lightly salted for a few hours to firm up a little, preventing it flaking apart when cooking. We serve this with some poached artichokes, clams steamed in white wine and some samphire, a zingy, slightly salty plant that can be gathered here on the shoreline in the west of Ireland if you know where to look!"

For 4
45 minutes preparation
60 minutes cooking

For the cod
400 g thick cod, skin and bones removed – a sharp knife and tweezers will do the job, as will a good fishmonger!
1 tablespoon sea salt crystals such as Maldon
Drizzle of sunflower oil
100 g butter

For the artichokes
4 firm long stem artichokes
100 ml olive oil
2 shallots sliced
2 cloves garlic sliced
1 slice smoked bacon
1 pinch fennel seeds
150 ml white wine
300ml chicken stock
1 tomato
1 lemon juiced
1 sprig fresh basil
Salt and pepper

In the morning, sprinkle the prepared cod with the sea salt, cover and refrigerate for a few hours. This will draw some moisture from the fish; the longer it sits the firmer the flesh will become.

Gently cook the sliced shallot, garlic and fennel seeds in the olive oil until softened.

Add the white wine along with the smoked bacon and continue cooking until half the wine has evaporated.

Add the chicken stock and seasoning, bring to a boil, remove from the heat and allow to cool.

Add the tomato, basil and lemon juice.

Remove the tough outside petals from an artichoke, then use a small, sharp knife to peel away all the tough skin.

Once peeled, pop it straight into the prepared stock. The lemon juice will help keep the flesh from turning brown.
Repeat this until all four artichokes are ready.

(continued)

Cut a piece of parchment to fit the size of the pot and place on top.

Bring to a simmer and cook for about 20 min or until just tender.

Remove from the heat and allow to cool in the stock, then refrigerate until needed. They will keep in the cooking stock (in the refrigerator) for 3 or 4 days.

To finish, rinse the excess salt from the cod, pat dry and divide into 4 even-sized pieces.

Heat a non-stick pan on a high heat and add a drizzle of sunflower oil.

When the oil is very hot, add the cod.

After 1 minute, the cod should start to brown, so turn the fish.

Add half the butter, and once it begins to foam, add the rest. Keep basting the fish with the butter, as it foams and turns nut brown, for about 2 or 3 min until the fish is cooked but still moist.

Transfer the cod to the plates and serve with the artichokes gently warmed in the cooking stock.

HERRING IN OATMEAL

A great, crunchy, buttery classic, and very good at breakfast time or for supper with some boiled potatoes, a poached egg and salad leaves. The best I've tasted was at The Woollen Mills café, overlooking the Ha'penny Bridge in Dublin.

For 4
5 minutes preparation
5 minutes cooking

4 fresh herring fillets
1 egg, beaten
4 tablespoons plain flour
250 g oatmeal
100 g melted butter
Juice of a lemon
Salt and pepper

Heat a little of the butter in a frying pan.
Season the flour with salt and pepper and spread it on a plate.
Dip the herrings in the flour, then the egg, then coat with the oatmeal.

Put the fillets flesh side down in the pan and cook for 2-3 minutes, turning once or twice until the fish is tender and the oatmeal golden.

Remove the fish from the pan, add the remaining butter and lemon juice, simmer together for a moment, then serve spooned over the warm fish.

SALMON AND OYSTER TARTARE WITH DILLISK AND LEMON

A lovely, easy, fresh way to start a summer dinner, this tartare is also excellent in smaller portions for drinks party nibbles, served in Little Gem leaves with gin cocktails or Guinness.

For 6 to 8
10 minutes preparation

400 g spanking fresh salmon, chilled, skinned
8 oysters
Sprinkling of dried dillisk
Zest and juice of a lemon

Cut the salmon into chunks.

Shuck the oysters, retaining their juice, and chop them.

Mix the salmon, oysters, oyster juice with the dillisk, lemon zest and juice.

Serve immediately.

WHITE FISH IN DARK BROTH WITH CLAMS

A much simplified version of a Dawn Perry recipe from the great *Bon Appetit* volumes, this dish is a little fiddly, not in terms of great cheffy know-how, but more in the number of saucepans and bits and pieces you'll need to pull it off and have it hot and fresh on the table for everyone at the same time. So I guess it is one rare occasion in my cooking where a *mise en place* is *de rigueur*, as they don't say in Ballymena.

And yes, I'm showing off a bit with the groovy buckshorn plantain. In the spirit of total disclosure, this foraged seashore gold was generously supplied to me by chef Stevie Toman of OX in Belfast, and it may be a tough item to find if you do not live by the seashore or go in much for picking your own food. You can replace its nutty taste and succulent texture with some young rocket or spinach leaves. The broth is not technically a broth, as it does not contain meat. But the meaty taste and colour the onions give it bring it pretty close in a fraction of the time.

For 4
1 hour preparation
15 minutes cooking

For the broth
4 medium onions, chopped
4 small carrots, peeled, chopped
Vegetable oil
1 garlic clove, peeled, crushed
1 bay leaf
Pepper corns

For the green sauce
Handful of flat-leaf parsley
1 spring onion (scallion)
Vegetable oil
Salt and pepper
4 boned pieces/chunks (about 175 g each) of firm, white fish (cod, hake, halibut)
About 2 dozen clams, scrubbed, any persistently open shells discarded
A small handful of buckshorn plantain or baby rocket leaves

Whizz the herbs with the oil in a mini processor and reserve. You will probably need to stir it again just before serving, so if you can manage to do this just before serving it will help the colour and the taste.

Pre-heat the oven to 180 °C. Toss the onions, garlic and carrots in oil and set them onto a baking sheet covered with foil. Roast for about 40 minutes or so, turning them as you go to make sure they brown but do not burn.

Put the roast vegetables into a comfortable saucepan and cover generously with boiling water (about 3 litres). Add the bayleaf and peppercorns and simmer gently for 40 minutes or so, until you start to have a tasty, coloured broth.

Strain the broth and reduce again to deepen the taste. You can prepare up until this step, then finish the dish 10 minutes before serving.

Once you have about 4 to 5 ladlefuls of broth, bring it to a fast simmer and throw in the scrubbed clams. Cover with a lid and let them bubble and steam for about 5 minutes, until all the shells are open. Remove the clams and keep them warm. Taste the broth and adjust the seasoning if you need to, the clams will make it salty.

MRS HEDERMAN'S HOT SMOKED SALMON FISHCAKES WITH CARROT, PARSLEY AND CELERY SEED BY CAROLINE HEDERMAN

The "secret" of our fishcakes is that we put plenty of Hederman smoked fish in them. They are essentially a mash or champ with smoked fish and a flavoured butter. You could use traditional smoked salmon, but I prefer the flaky texture of our hot smoked salmon.

The flavour in this particular recipe also depends on very good carrots (ours are from Ballintubber Farm) – otherwise use another sweet roast veg. I use Macroom stone-ground oatmeal to coat the fishcakes – it's lovely and nutty and softer than the other un-ground varieties, but you can use breadcrumb or a simple dusting of flour.

For 4 to 6
20 minutes preparation
10 minutes cooking

500 g cooked, mashed floury potatoes e.g. Roosters or Kerr's Pink
250 g flaked, hot smoked fish
150 g thickly grated carrot
1 level teaspoon (or more) of celery seed
80 g butter
Juice of a lemon, or grated rind of an organic one
1-2 grated garlic cloves
Big handful of chopped flat-leaf parsley
Stone-ground oatmeal for coating

Gently cook the garlic and carrot in the butter for about 4-5 minutes, so that the carrots still have a bit of bite, but the butter has taken on a golden hue, and the garlic has lost its raw edge. Add celery seed for the last minute or so, and the lemon at the end. Then combine the potato, fish, flavoured butter and chopped parsley until well mixed. Use more butter or a little milk if the mixture is at all dry. Divide mixture into 4-6 and shape into fishcakes, coat in oatmeal and pan fry in a little butter and rapeseed/olive oil. Approximately 4-5 minutes on each side at a moderate heat should do it.

Sea spaghetti on the beach at Strandhill, Co. Sligo

LEMON SOLE WITH SHRIMP, BROWN BUTTER AND CUCUMBER SAUCE, BY DEREK CREAGH, HARRY'S BRIDGEND

For 4
10 minutes preparation
20 minutes cooking

4 lemon sole, skinned
Groundnut oil
150 g potted brown shrimp, shop bought
5 g flat-leaf parsley chopped
½ lemon (juiced)
½ cucumber, deseeded, halved and sliced
100 g brown butter
Sea salt

Heat the groundnut oil in a non-stick frying pan over a medium heat. Place the sole in the pan.

Fry until golden brown before carefully turning the whole fish over. Continue frying for a further 3-4 min.

Remove the whole fish from the pan and place on a baking tray lined with parchment paper and put into oven for about 5 min.

Remove any oil from the pan and add 2-3 tablespoons of water to deglaze the pan.

Add brown shrimp, lemon juice and brown butter and warm gently until hot, then add cucumber and chopped parsley.

Remove fish from oven and place onto warm plates, check seasoning and then spoon over shrimp, cucumber and brown butter sauce.

HEDERMAN'S SMOKED SALMON WITH SMOKED CRÈME FRAÎCHE

A million apologies if you do not possess a smoke-making contraption, for, until Frank and Caroline Hederman (who introduced me to the idea) sell their own, smoked cream is a tough enough commodity to find in the shops. I try to avoid cheffy gadgets myself, but I gave in to a smoking gun, having received an in-person butter smoking tutorial from the lovely Robbie Krawczyk at Tankardstown house.

We (the gun and I) are still very much in our honeymoon phase. I love how handy it is to direct the smoke into a container with small amounts of food.

For 4
30 minutes preparation

200 g crème fraîche or whipped double cream

Put the cream in a wide bowl and spread it out on the bottom to increase its surface. Direct the smoke into the bowl and close it firmly with cling film wrapped all around. Leave to infuse a good 20 minutes or so. Then put the cream into a bowl and seal it again until you are ready to serve it with the smoked salmon.

SHERIDANS BROWN BREAD CRACKERS WITH PEPPERS AND SMOKED SALMON

Fast approaching cult status, now sold all over the world, these tasty crackers are brilliant with cheese and even better with the little combination below.

For 10 crackers or so
30 minutes cooking
5 minutes preparation

200 g smoked salmon
200 g cream cheese (Kilbeg Dairies would do very nicely)
20 young nettle leaves

Juice of 1 lemon
1 red pepper

Roast the pepper under a grill until completely black all over, put in a bowl cover and with cling film. This helps to remove skin.

Blanch the nettle leaves for 5 seconds in boiling water , remove and place in a bowl of cold water (this takes away the sting of the nettle). Drain, pat dry with kitchen paper and chop finely.
Remove the pepper skin by simply rubbing off by hand or with some kitchen paper. Remove seeds and chop in to bite size pieces.

Mix together nettles, pepper, cream cheese and lemon juice.
Spread the crackers with a little nettle pepper cheese, and set some salmon on top. Garnish with pea shoots or anything green and pretty.

Maghera Beach near Ardara, Co. Donegal.

PEARL BARLEY WITH MACKEREL, HAZELNUTS, BURNT APPLE AND PICKLED SAMPHIRE

I'm a little embarrassed to confess that this is the first dish (to my knowledge) which ever made one of my guests physically ill. Please do not be alarmed. It is, though I say it myself, perfectly delicious, it's just that the guest in question, being possibly the most traditional Irishman I have ever met, was also too polite to mention his aversion to mackerel.

Fish in general, and strong, oily mackerel in particular, are not the most loved of foods in rural Ireland, where there is still a firm squeamishness, bordering on disgust, about them, especially in the summer months when there is a seasonal glut. It was about as distasteful to my guest as Mummie's rabbit mousse had been in Molly Keane's *Good Behaviour*.

I didn't realize. I do now.

But the flakes of fresh mackerel here, I promise, make for a very good dish if you are brave enough. Barley gives a terrific risotto-ish texture and taste and the pickled samphire a tart freshness most people love. You could also use salmon, trout, or a mixture of all three. The barley needs a good oily, meaty fish to stand up to it here, and some asparagus, salad leaves or green beans would certainly be welcome too.

For 4
15 minutes preparation
40 minutes cooking

2 shallots or 1 onion finely chopped
30 g butter or a little oil
300 g pearl barley
1 litre hot chicken or vegetable stock
20 g butter
4 fresh mackerel fillets
2 cooking apples, peeled, cored, cut into chunks
4 heaped teaspoons pickled samphire (or fresh samphire)
A small handful of crushed hazelnuts, toasted.
Salt and pepper
Lemon juice

Melt the butter in a saucepan and sweat the onion over a low heat until it is soft. Add the barley and cook for a few minutes until pouring in the stock and bringing to a low simmer. Season lightly and cook for about 30 minutes or so, stirring until the barley is soft and has absorbed most of the liquid. You might have to top up with some water if it is too thick.

While the barley is cooking, fry the apples in a non stick pan until they are nicely blackened and caramelized on one side. Take them out of the pan and keep them warm.

Season and keep the cooked barley warm as you cook the fish.

Fry or grill the mackerel fillets and flake the flesh into small bite size pieces.

Serve stirred through the barley, garnished with the samphire and some hazelnuts. Give it all a few drops of fresh lemon juice to liven the dish up before serving.

ROBBIE KRAWCZYK

In Ireland "humble" is an often overused way of describing talented and successful people who, not quite realizing how talented they are, do not tend to brag about their success. I'm betting that the softly spoken, art school graduate ROBBIE KRAWCZYK will have the word "humble" tacked to his name again and again over the next few years, as foodlovers discover his fine dining menu at Trish Conroy's masterclass in grown-up hospitality, Tankardstown House.

Perfectly versed in the current New Nordic gastro codes of pickling, smoking, curing (Robbie's father is Irish charcuterie pioneer Frank Krawczyk) and foraging – which sit so well with Irish produce and cooking traditions when used with wit and intelligence – Robbie's beautiful dishes include the obligatory on-trend touches of spherification, dehydration, micro leaves, crispy chicken skin and slow-cooked egg yolks, yet rarely does he loosen his grip on flavour.

Like his first mentor, Richard Corrigan, Robbie was raised with the pure and simple excellence of home-grown Irish ingredients. His West Cork childhood (his parents grew their own organic vegetables) meant that the proper taste of things was forever imprinted on his palate. And it is this, more than anything else, which shines through his sparky, super-accomplished cooking.

SEASHORE,
BY ROBBIE KRAWCZYK
AT TANKARDSTOWN HOUSE

For 4 to 6
5 minutes preparation time
25 cooking preparation time

For the ceviche of monkfish
50 g monkfish
1 lemon
1 lime and zest
Pinch dried chili and one of sea salt
20 ml olive oil

For the ink emulsion
1 egg
1/2 tea spoon Dijon mustard
10 g squid ink
200 ml sunflower oil

For the edible sand
20 g prawn oil
Maltose to mix
Toasted bread crumbs
1/2 teaspoon scallop roe powder
1/2 teaspoon black pudding crumbs
Salt and pepper
Cucumber jelly
1 cucumber peeled
100 g cured mackerel
100 g fresh squid tentacles
50 g smoked eel

For the garnish
Seaweed, samphire, ice lettuce, herring roe, fennel tops

For the ceviche of monkfish, slice the monkfish and marinate in the remaining ingredients for 2 hours. Grill the squid tentacles.

For the ink emulsion, place egg yolk and mustard in a bowl and whisk together slowly, then steadily whisk in oil, being careful not to add it too quickly or it will split. Once emulsified, add ink, then season and place in a small piping bag.

With a blow torch char the cucumber until black. And for the edible sand, mix all ingredients to achieve desired effect. Arrange all the elements on the plate.

Finish with seaweed, samphire, ice lettuce, herring roe and fennel tops.

BACON,
PORK,
SAUSAGES
AND PUDDINGS

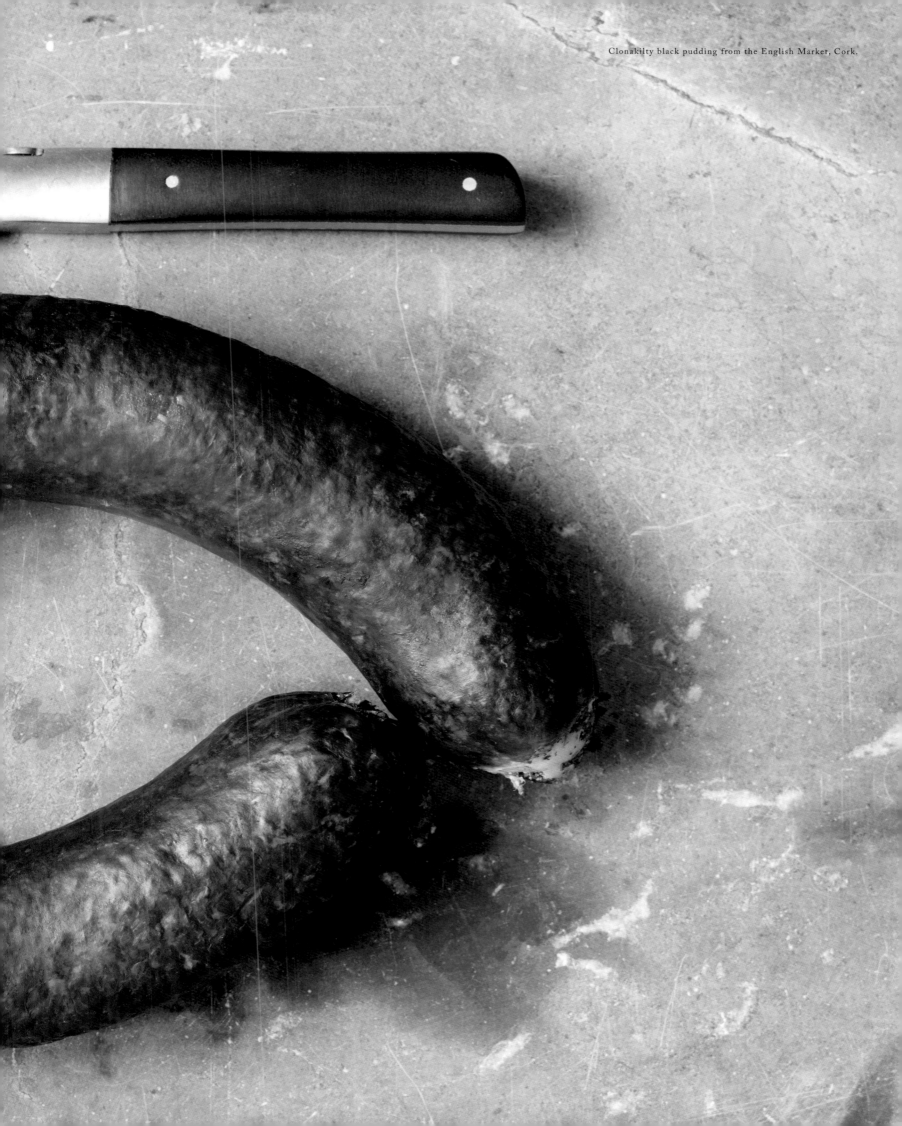

Clonakilty black pudding from the English Market, Cork.

THE FULL IRISH BREAKFAST AND THE ULSTER FRY

"A full Irish feels like that one Christmas where you got everything you wanted. It feels like watching the silhouette of a wolf, stood stark in contrast, howling at the moon. It smells like new baby smell, new car smell, and €1,000 all rolled into one. It is the mother of your child, the end of the Cornetto, and the cigarette after sex." Anon. (sadly), Ireland.

Borders aside, there are so many variations and quirks around our national breakfast that there is no point in trying to declare one version tastier or more authentic than another. Everyone has a preference, and even if we all agree (more or less) on bacon, sausage, black and white puddings and egg as the four cornerstones, fried potatoes, mushrooms, baked beans* and tomatoes come and go from plates up and down the country.

That said, there are two main differences between an Irish and an Ulster breakfast fry-up. Firstly, well before the arrival of the wonderful, hangover busting All Day Breakfast, we Northerners had no shame whatsoever about serving it for tea. High Tea, that is, at 6 o'clock, hence the crafty non mealtime-specific title. A teatime Ulster Fry near Ballyclare can very easily stray into Mixed Grill territory by including a lamb chop, or a piece of that sausage-like indigestible oddity made with invisible leeks, carrots and onions, the vegetable roll.

The other difference between Irish and Ulster breakfasts is the amount of bread on the plate or in the pan. An Ulster Fry will always have fried soda and/or potato bread, and often, a fried sweet pancake. Personally, and this is not merely childhood conditioning speaking, I find this a complete stroke of genius. The fried breads, far superior to awkward buttered toast or crumbly soda bread on the side, provide the perfect warm sponge for a runny egg or a juicy tomato and take on their own lovely flavour as they absorb the fat from the sausage, pudding and bacon. And the sweet pancake's value, next to crispy bacon, needs no justification to anyone who has ever enjoyed bacon and pancakes US style.

There are many elaborate "recipes" for producing the best Irish cooked breakfast, many of them using ovens, grills and multiple pans and sometimes, God forbid, a deep fat fryer. When I am being cooked for in a hotel or an Irish B&B, I do prefer a poached egg to a fried one, but at home that is just too much effort and co-ordination for too little pleasure, too early in the morning.

If there are two or more of you for breakfast, you might have to use two pans, or even have the grill going for bacon (though you will miss out on the delicious, lubrifying fat), but a lot of unhelpful instruction is given, I believe, by chefs with unlimited kit and staff, or cooks showing off slightly by trying to make things more complicated than they are. It is breakfast, not gastronomy. Just as in many of the recipes in my book (Seamus Hogan's Bacon and Cabbage being the perfect example) the most important part of the work, choosing good produce, will be done before you even take your pan from the cupboard.

Here I've given the ingredients and the order in which to cook them in one pan, for an Ulster Fry for two people.

*Overheard in a rebel country guesthouse: "Michael Collins would be turning in his grave to see baked beans on a full Irish…"

THE ULSTER FRY

For 2
15 minutes cooking

Vegetable oil
A knob of butter
2 sausages
4 rashers bacon (streaky or back bacon)
2 pieces of potato bread
2 pancakes
A few cherry tomatoes, cut in half
2 eggs

Heat the oil with the butter and when it starts to sizzle slightly, add the sausages. Cook them for about 5 minutes, at a nice medium heat, turning them once or twice so they brown all over.

Once they are nicely on the go, add the bacon and let it crisp up. Turn once after a minute or so.

Now add the bread, pancakes and tomatoes and let it all cook together. Turning once but not moving things around too much.

Finally, once everything is golden and cooked through, move it aside in the pan and break in the eggs. If you do not have room, do them one at a time, removing the other elements if they are cooked through. You might prefer a completely clean pan for the eggs. If that's the case, remove the sausages, bacon and breads, keep them warm, give the pan a quick wash and use fresh oil to fry the eggs.

Serve piping hot with tea or coffee and buttered toast and marmalade.

BACON AND CABBAGE BY SEAMUS HOGAN

Have a warm, strawed shed ready, as well as an ample trough and access to fresh water.

Then choose an old breed of pig — I am partial to Saddlebacks — and buy two Bonhams of the same sex that are 10 weeks old and have been weaned at least two weeks already. Do not buy pigs without teeth or tails! Above all, buy from a reputable breeder.

And don't be afraid to chat about your project. Most pig people love to talk about pigs. For example, you will need to know what the piglets have been fed on up to this time, as a sudden change of diet for a young pig is often fatal.

Why two pigs, one might ask? Well, almost all animals are social and none more so than pigs. If you are passing a field of cattle tomorrow will they run over to you and chat? No, they will not. But pigs will. So two is company.

Returning to the shed. It is important that the pigs have access to a run where they can get out and root. Nowadays this is a great deal easier with the use of an electric fence.

If you are new to rearing pigs, what will strike you first is that the expression "Like a pig in shit" is a load of, well, shit. They are, I think, the cleanest of our domestic animals, and when possible will always go outside to go if they can.

I am no gardener, so if you are like me, then team up with someone who is greenfingered and decide on which variety of floury potato you wish to grow to accompany your bacon and cabbage. The latter, for best results, can only be of the York type, maybe Durham Early? A row of these are a work of art in any garden.

Even though it is a long way away, the day will come when your pigs will become pork and bacon and sausages and puddings and all manner of wonderful things, so get yourself a copy of Jane Grigson's *Charcuterie And French Pork Cookery*. It is also a good thing to prevent one from getting too attached to one's pigs. They do make great pals, so be careful.

We can now skip to the point where the potatoes and cabbage are ready and your pigs have moved to the barrel, the fridge and the freezer. If you want, you can cure your own bacon, but I found a butcher that cured mine for me.* Any piece of mild cured bacon will be lovely, but I find that a piece of bacon from the belly — streaky bacon as it is called — is the tastiest at the end of the day.

For two people, a pound of bacon should be plenty. A few slices cut from the piece before cooking is very nice next morning fried with a freshly laid egg.

Cut your head of cabbage in two and remove the core. Discard the outer leaves but not all the green leaves. This colour is very lovely I think in the finished dish. Place the cabbage in a saucepan, and onto this place the bacon. I like my cabbage well cooked. Around the bacon, place four potatoes (more if there are big appetites) and pour enough water into the pot to just cover the potatoes and bacon. Some people put the potatoes on a steaming device over the bacon and cabbage. Some cook them completely separately depending on the potato type and size. Bring to the boil and simmer gently until the potatoes are cooked — or "smiling", as I have heard my mother describe them. Then remove the potatoes and bacon and place on a warm plate and cover with a dish cloth.

Drain most, but not all, of the water from the cabbage, leaving a few tablespoons for taste. Toss in a lump of butter and chop up the cabbage, but not too finely. Slice your bacon thinly, not skinny, and serve with the potatoes, cabbage and lots of lovely butter. And a pinch of salt on the potatoes is a must. In Cork, people are said to "Ate their spuds, skins an all". I have not seen it myself.

*O Connell's, Little Catherine St. Limerick.

WHITE SAUCE WITH PARSLEY

I'm sorry for the slight finger-wagging here, but this is so incredibly easy to make, and make very well, that I cannot understand why cooks resort so often to packet imitations. It has all the simple, good things that go so well with Irish bacon : milk, butter, parsley, thyme. It just needs a bit of whisking and a little last minute care.

Once you master the technique you will have added bechamel sauce to your repertoire, meaning all sorts of gratins are now within your reach. Simply add good characterful cheese in the sauce, and on top of the dish, for delicious cauliflower, kale, cabbage or chard gratin.

For 4
5 minutes cooking

50 g butter
1 tablespoon flour
500 ml fresh milk
2 tablespoons fresh curly or flat-leaf parsley
A pinch of thyme

In a saucepan, non-stick is best, cook the flour and the butter together, mixing with a wooden spoon, to make a smooth paste.

Add a little milk and whisk to smooth out the mixture.

Slowly add the rest of the milk and bring to the boil, whisking to avoid any lumps.

Simmer for a minute or two. If it is too thick, add a little more milk.

Season with salt and pepper, add the herbs and let them infuse before serving with bacon and cabbage.

If you are making ahead, set cling film over the surface of the hot sauce until you are ready to reheat it. This will stop a skin forming.

Caper sauce.

This is very good with poached leg of mutton. Simply add a handful of drained capers and a good tablespoon of mustard to the white sauce recipe.

BALLYVOLANE HOUSE, FERMOY, CO. CORK

Ballyvolane House is a little piece of Irish paradise, with, befittingly, a couple of angels acting as your hosts. It's a grand old house, with a long and illustrious history, but it exudes warmth, peace, comfort and fun! Staying here is a sort of *Swallows and Amazons* meets *Downton Abbey* experience, only instead of frowsty dowagers at the door you get Justin and Jenny Green, the most handsome, charming couple in County Cork (probably in all of Ireland, let's face it). As well as the beautifully decorated bedrooms in the main house, you can camp in luxurious *Out of Africa* style on the lawns. Justin and Jenny have transformed many of the farm buildings, making an incredibly romantic and funky wedding or party venue, complete with big barn and a very cool bar.

The walled garden has been restored and provides the house's kitchens with fresh fruit and veg, whilst ducks, chickens and rare breed pigs help make Ballyvolane's breakfasts so good. During the salmon season, Ballyvolane is also a very much sought-after venue for keen fishermen. I was lucky enough to stay here a few years ago, for several weeks in off-season, while filming for RTE, just as Justin and Jenny were getting the business up and running; and I experienced first hand their incredible energy and hospitality. A special place, and one of the most quietly luxurious experiences Ireland has to offer.

Top left: Jenny and Justin Green outside Ballyvolane house.

IRISH LITTLE GEM, GUBBEEN WILD VENISON SALAMI, CIDER VINEGAR AND RAPESEED OIL VINAIGRETTE

Irish Little Gems are larger, frillier and tastier than those I have become used to in France. A mini version of Cos salads, they are perfect for plating, as their long, naturally cupped leaves stay fresh and firm.
In this recipe, they are also a good backdrop to Fingal Ferguson's wonderful charcuterie from the celebrated Gubbeen farm, one of Ireland's pioneering producers, set in a "gentle and fertile corner of West Cork".

Here I have teamed sweet apples and grassy Donegal rapeseed oil with Gubbeen's wild venison salami; it is both fruity and earthy, smoked over "sweet woods" and cooked in white wine. Add a few fried bacon chunks for a bit of crunch and you'll have a great salad starter or light lunch.

For 2
5 minutes preparation

1 Irish little gem, leaves removed, washed and spun
About 50 or 60 g of Gubbeen wild venison salami, sliced finely
50 g bacon chunks
1 eating apple, sliced finely
3 tablespoons Irish rapeseed oil
1 tablespoon cider vinegar
Salt and pepper

Set the salad leaves on two large plates. Dot the salami over them.

Fry the bacon until crisp, then scatter it and the apple slices evenly over the leaves. Drizzle with a vinaigrette made from the oil and vinegar, and seasoned with salt and pepper.

Serve immediately with some good soda bread and salted butter.

POTATO OAT CAKES WITH BACON STEAKS

Easy to make, crunchy and nutritious, "pratie oatens" are lovely with good Irish bacon and gammon. As ever, no stinting on the butter.

For 6
5 minutes preparation
25 minutes cooking

1 kg floury potatoes
75 g porridge oats
50 g flour
100 g butter
Salt and pepper

Peel and boil the potatoes until they are soft, and mash them with 70 g or so of the butter.

Mix in the oats (leaving a tablespoon to coat the cakes) and flour, season with salt and pepper and form the mixture into 6 rounds.

Press the remaining oats into the surface of the cakes.

Heat the butter in a non-stick pan and cook the oatcakes until they are crispy and golden on the outside.

WHISKEY BACON CARAMEL PORRIDGE

Mildly over the top, I guess, this little breakfast concoction, and definitely close to hair-of-the-dog hangover remedy territory. It also doesn't look that fabulous, but made of all the best Irish things, what ca go wrong?

For 2
5 minutes preparation
10 minutes cooking, if that

4 tablespoons porridge oats
200 ml fresh milk
2 thick cut rashers, chopped, or 2 tablespoons of bacon lardons
1 level tablespoon Demerara sugar
A dash of whiskey
2 tablespoons cream (plus more for pouring, possibly)

Make the porridge with the milk and keep it warm.

Heat a frying pan and fry the bacon. When it starts to sizzle and render a little fat, sprinkle the sugar on stir to coat. Let it caramelise for a few minutes before adding the dash of whiskey to deglaze the pan.

As it bubbles and evaporates, scrape all the fried, caramel bacon bits from the pan and then pour in the cre

Stir it all again until nicely mixed and serve over the hot porridge, with extra cream. Go on.

PORK BRINED IN CIDER WITH BAYLEAVES

Use only free range, organic pork here. It is not easy to find these days but, thankfully, in Ireland, free range farms, such as Woodside in Cork and Olde Farm in Tipperary, are making a comeback. Likewise our craft apple juices and ciders, so both are celebrated in this celebration dish.

For 6 to 8
10 minutes preparation
1 night's brining
1 hour 15 cooking

200 g light brown sugar
175 g salt
8 bay leaves
1 tablespoon black peppercorns ground coarsely
1 litre good Irish apple cider
1 pork loin roast (5 lbs about)
Olive oil

Put the sugar, salt, pepper, 300 ml of water and 2 bay leaves into a saucepan and let them dissolve over a medium heat. Pour the brine into a large bowl, add the cider and leave it to cool.

Put the pork and the brine into a very large re-sealable freezer bag, seal and leave to chill in the fridge overnight.

Remove the pork from the bag, pat it dry and let it come up to room temperature (about 30 minutes).

Pre-heat the oven to 220 °C.

Brown the pork all over in a little oil, either in a pan, or in the roasting tin itself on the hob.

Tuck the remaining bay leaves under the string and put the pork in the oven for about 1 hour and 15 minutes.

Let the roast rest for a good 20 minutes before carving and serving.

SOUP MIX SOUP WITH BACON BITS, MACROOM FLOUR BREAD AND SEAWEED BUTTER

The "soup mix" I remember from my childhood kitchen cupboards was a mixture of pearl barley, split red lentils, and green and yellow split peas, used to thicken up the broth from a boiler chicken, very often served with boiled potatoes in their jackets, for Saturday lunches on our farm.

This way of transforming humble broth into a substantial stew capable of satisfying even my gigantic children has stuck with me over the years, and the little packets have been frequent stowaways in my luggage back from Ireland over the years.

Here the wonder-pulses are all fancied up with fried bacon bits and toasted soda bread crumbs on top and Macroom soda bread from The English Market in Cork with seaweed butter on the side.
Serve it as a hearty weekday supper dish, or on a big table with oysters or prawns for guests when you feel like dropping the beef or lamb for once.

For 6 to 8
2 hours 10 preparation
30 minutes cooking

A good pot of stock made from a boiler chicken, 2 carrots, 2 onions, 1 stick of celery
Boiled for 2 hours
250 g soup mix
Salt and pepper
200 g bacon lardons
2 or 3 slices soda farl or soda bread, made into breadcrumbs
30 g butter for frying
100 g butter, softened
4 tablespoons dried seaweed (kelp, Kombu, dillisk)

Rehydrate the seaweed if needs be. Drain and mix it into the softened butter with a fork.

Strain the chicken stock, retaining pieces of meat if you like. They will add texture but will be tasteless.

Reduce it to about 3 litres by simmering and season lightly before adding the soup mix. Simmer for about 20 minutes until the pulses are soft and have absorbed the chicken taste.

Season again with salt and pepper and keep warm.

Fry the bacon in the pan with the butter and the bread crumbs until everything is nice and crispy and golden.

Serve the soup with the bacon and soda bread as a garnish and the bread and butter on the side.

Alternatively, for a few calories saved, you can forget about the bread and bacon altogether and simply melt a small knob of seaweed butter into the soup.

LIVER AND BACON
WITH MASH AND
CIDER-BRAISED ONIONS

I once heard Irish actor Gabriel Byrne comment that to make their mark, all Irish writers had to "first get James Joyce off their backs". I wonder if this is how some young and ambitious Irish chefs wanting to champion Irish food abroad might feel too. How difficult it must be to shake off the vivid images Joyce painted in many minds of our hearty but heavy food, particularly in Dublin ? It's certainly Bloom's meal in *Ulysees*, of cider, mashed potatoes, bacon and liver slices at the Ormond Hotel that makes this dish say "Dublin" so clearly to me even though I have never eaten it there.

If you want to go the whole Ulyseean hog, Bloomsday or not, *The Joyce of Cooking* by Alison Armstrong (Station Hill Press, 1986) is great fun. She has meticulously extracted all the food from Joyce's writing and has constructed recipes around it, giving us gems like "Curly Cabbage a la Duchesse de Parme", "Lizzie Twig's Don't Eat a Beef Steak Nut Steak and Tomato Surprise" and "Protestant Soup".

For 4
10 minutes preparation
25 minutes cooking

4 slices calf's liver
4 slices back bacon
1 kg fluffy potatoes
75 g butter
Salt and pepper

For the onions
30 g butter
1 large onion
300 ml cider
Salt and pepper

Peel and boil the potatoes for 20 minutes until they are soft.

Mash them with butter and a little hot milk if you like and keep warm.

While the potatoes are cooking, melt the butter in the pan and start to fry the onions.

Season lightly and cook on a gentle heat until they soften and begin to brown.

Add the cider, stir and let the onions simmer gently for 5 minutes or so until most of the liquid has reduced.

Remove from the pan and keep warm.

Heat a little more butter in the pan and fry the liver until it is slightly crispy at the edges and still a little pink inside. Fry or grill the bacon until it is crispy. Season the onions before serving with the mash, liver and bacon.

Harland and Wolff cranes, Belfast.

GAMMON STEAKS, CIDER GLAZE, OAT AND POTATO CAKES WITH DULSE

Leftover mashed potato can never go back to its delectable fluffiness once reheated, especially when it has been left to cool right down. So it is much more advisable, to resurrect it in some new form, preferably involving some crunch, or at least crispiness. Adding oats and some seaweed brings extra oomph and texture if your spuds have gone a little flabby – as is their wont. Alongside a thick slice of Irish, free range, organic (the only way to go with pork in these days) or largely cruel, industrialised production gammon, fried and deglazed in tart cider vinegar and sweet apple juice, these potato cakes are just right.

For 4
10 minutes preparation
20 minutes cooking

Around 300 g cold mashed potato
2 tablespoons rolled oats
1 tablespoon dulse flakes
Pepper
50 g butter
1 tablespoon olive oil
4 gammon steaks, organic if possible, free range at least
50 g butter
1 tablespoon olive oil
1 tablespoon cider vinegar
1 small glass of fresh apple juice

Mix the potato with the dulse and the oats, season with pepper and fashion into 4 to 6 potato cakes of about 1½ cm thickness. Leave them at room temperature.

Heat the oil with a knob of the butter and fry the gammon steaks until they are nicely caramelized. Remove from the pan, cover them and keep them warm.

Deglaze the pan with the vinegar and scrape up the cooking juices. Add the apple juice and reduce until you have a good syrupy sauce. Pop the gammon back in the pan and keep the whole thing warm while you are cooking the potato cakes.

In another frying pan, heat the butter and oil and fry the potato cakes until they are golden and crispy on all sides.

Serve immediately with the warm gammon and the sauce.

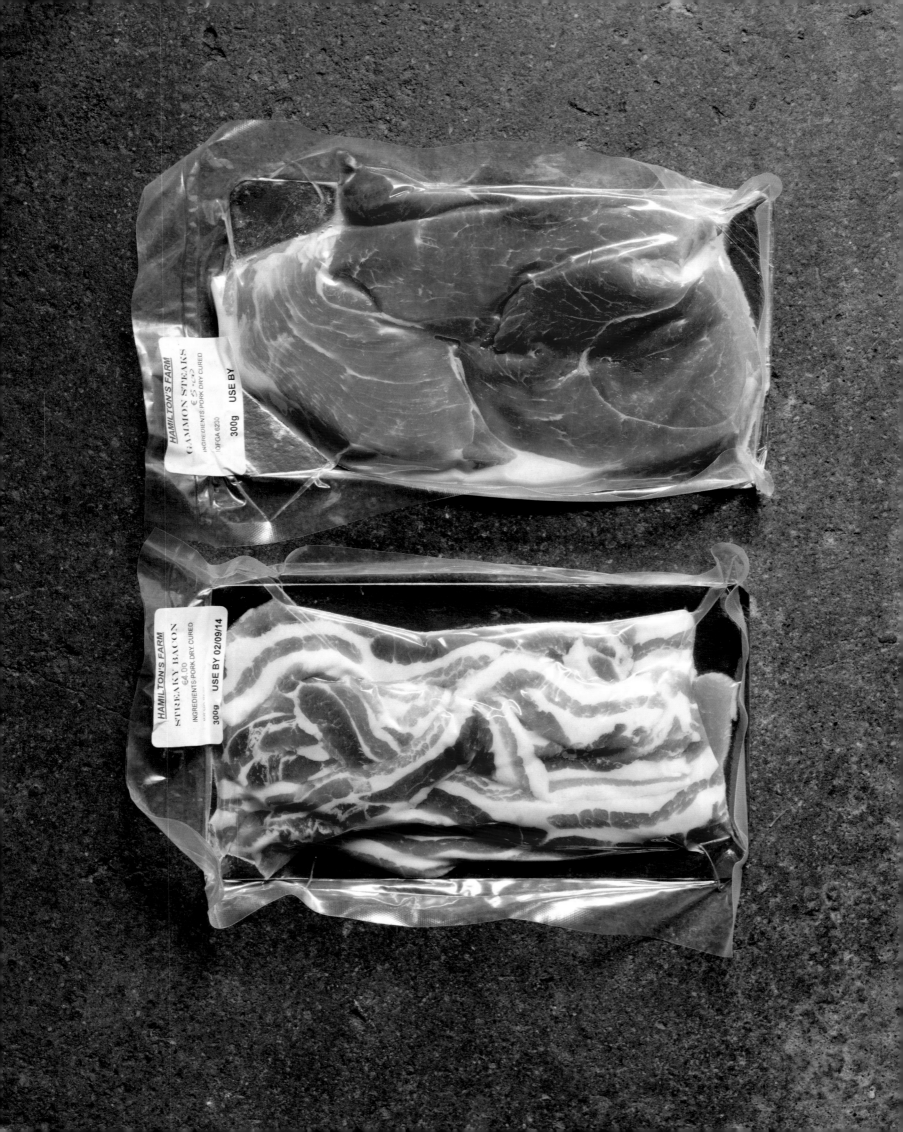

DUBLIN CODDLE

You simply cannot write a book about Irish cooking and not include this ancient, historical Irish dish. Photographing it is another matter, however, as it is basically sausages and ham simmered for a long time, with onions, potatoes and parsley, making a sort of gloopy, oniony stew with pink meat which, despite the long cook, stubbornly looks raw. I first tasted it only a year or so ago, in Dublin's very hip The Woollen Mills – and very satisfying it was.

Just like Irish stew, there is fierce debate around any tampering with the original version of this dish. A lot of browning of the bacon and sausages goes on, in an attempt to make the stew a little more attractive, and often cooks will slip a carrot or two, or even some Guinness, in the pot alongside the potatoes.

When I tried making this filling dish at home, I can't say it was a huge success with my half-French children; after all, they have some magnificent French pork-based stews (cassoulet, potée, choucroute, to name but a few) with which to compare it. But the point of Coddle is sustenance, not gastronomy, and even if it doesn't tempt you enough to become part of your usual repertoire, it is certainly worth a bash on historical grounds the next time you are cooking a St Patrick's or Bloomsday feast.

For 4 to 6
10 minutes preparation
2 hours cooking

8 slices, thickly cut Irish bacon or ham (free range, organic if possible)
8 or 10 Irish pork sausages (free range, organic if possible)
4 or 5 onions, peeled, sliced
1 kg firm potatoes, peeled, sliced
Salt and pepper
Fresh parsley

Pre-heat the oven to 150 °C.

Bring a litre of water to the boil in a medium sized saucepan. Poach the bacon and sausages in it for about 5 minutes. Drain the meat and reserve the poaching liquid.

Place the sausages and bacon into a heavy-based (lidded) casserole, mix with the potatoes, onions, half the parsley and enough of the poaching liquid to cover it all. Season lightly as the bacon and sausages are already salty.

Theodora tells us to cut a circle of greaseproof paper and set it over the meat and potatoes, before putting the lid on the casserole, but you can skip this and let the coddle cook quietly in its pot — for 1½ hours.

Garnish with the remaining parsley and serve steaming hot with buttered soda bread and plenty of Guinness.

GRAHAM NEVILLE

Dublin — vibrant, busy, ever food-loving Dublin — is home to the very swish and exclusive Restaurant Forty One, tucked inside the private members' club Residence, one of the most famous relics (now under new ownership), of the Celtic Tiger — the giddy times of economic boom (1995-2007), when credit was cheap and house prices soared. Head Chef GRAHAM NEVILLE joined Residence in 2008 after spending a number of years working in Chicago, cooking progressive French cuisine at both Tru and Les Nomades and rubbing shoulders with legendary chef Charlie Trotter. When he returned to Ireland, he worked for seven years at Michelin starred Thornton's in Dublin. His style is opulent enough to do the luxurious surroundings justice, yet firmly rooted in a desire to lift his classical command of textures and ingredients with more modern touches that bring his dishes together. Sauces steer away from the cream and butter still so dear to Dubliners' hearts. Neville prefers to make the most of vegetable and fruit juices, many of which come from produce grown in the restaurant's very own organic walled kitchen garden just outside the city. Graham is a keen forager, something that is *de rigueur* for any young chef these days, bringing back herbs (sea purslane, lovage, gorse flowers) and seaweed from walks along the coast, which often find their way onto diners' plates. He's a champion of local, seasonal Irish produce and marries it beautifully with many touches of French luxury on his accomplished and decadent tasting menu.

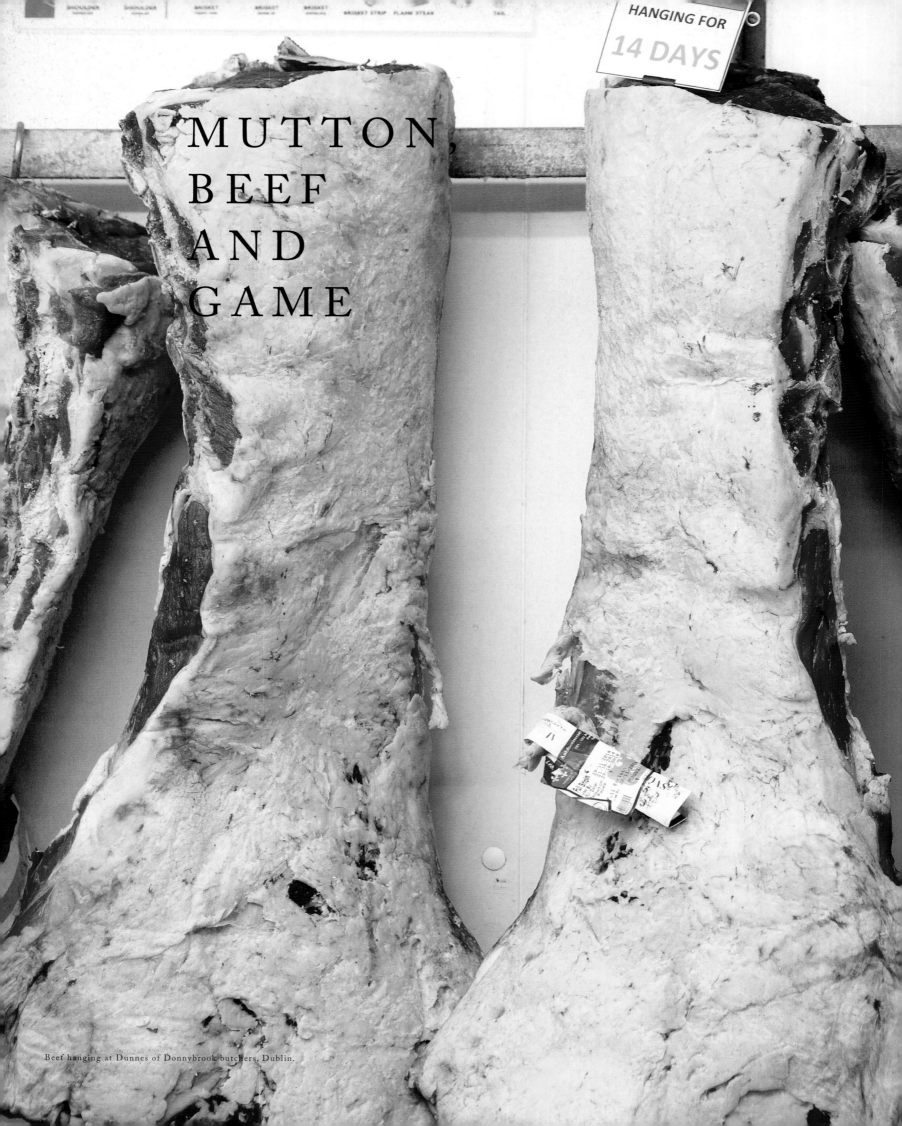

MUTTON,
BEEF
AND
GAME

Beef hanging at Dunnes of Donnybrook butchers, Dublin.

SUNDAY ROAST BEEF

This magnificent beast (or this part of it), a Hereford, comes from Donnes butchers in a busy foodie quarter of Dublin, Donnybrook.

Irish beef is predominantly grass-fed, and although its quality and the sustainability of its production might be threatened by the domination of "efficient" giant Simmental and Charolais breeds — feeding demand from international markets — much is being done within the country to slow the cereal feed invasion and inform about the advantages of fatter, marbled meat from smaller breeds, including Angus, Hereford and Shorthorn as well as Irish natives such as Dexters and Irish Moiled.

This is one of the very few places in the book where I have used garlic — trying as I am to keep to as "old" Irish ingredients as possible. But really, here it would be a sin not to simply enhance the wonderful taste of the meat in this simple way.

For 8
10 minutes preparation
1½ hours cooking

Sea salt
Olive oil
2 garlic cloves
5 kg or so fore-rib of beef, French trimmed, rolled and tied
Salt and pepper

Preheat the oven to 200 °C.

Rub the joint with the split garlic cloves, a little salt and olive oil. Roast for 1½ hours (for medium rare meat) in a large roasting tray, adding the potatoes (if you have room) for the final 30 minutes.

Leave to rest for 20 minutes before carving.

GLAZED CARROTS

For 6
10 minutes preparation
25 minutes cooking

8 or 10 carrots
47g butter
2 teaspoons sugar
A dash of lemon or orange juice

Steam the peeled carrots until tender but not too soft.

Heat 75 g butter with 2 teaspoons sugar and a dash of lemon or orange in a wide pan. Coat the carrots with the sweet butter to glaze.

Season with salt and pepper and serve with the beef and potatoes.

POTATOES ROASTED
IN BEEF DRIPPING

For 6
20 minutes preparation
45 minutes cooking

2 kg Desiree or rooster potatoes, peeled, cut into chunks
150 g beef dripping

Pre-heat the oven to 220 °C.

Put the fat in a roasting tray and pre-heat, as the oven temperature rises. Par-boil the potatoes for 10 minutes. The outer edge should be fluffy but the inside still hard. Drain off the water, hold the lid onto the saucepan and shake the potatoes vigorously to roughen the edges. This is the secret to making them especially crunchy once cooked.

Take the roasting tray from the oven (be careful!) and set it on the hob. Using a long handled spoon, put the potataoes into the hot fat, taking care not to splash yourself. Move the tray around so that the potatoes are completely coated in the fat. Put the tray back into the oven and roast for 45 minutes until they are golden brown.

Take them out, sprinkle with a little salt and serve right away with the rested, warm beef and glazed carrots.

BUTCHER PAT WHELAN ON THE GREAT DRIPPING COMEBACK

"Dripping, as the name suggests, is the fat that drips from meat as it cooks. When I speak of dripping I would always mean beef dripping. If you cook a roast of beef, the joint juices left in the pan when you remove the meat is effectively dripping. If you were to let it cool it would solidify into a white substance. We usually pour off all but a few teaspoons of this hot liquid fat and add it to the other ingredients to make gravy. If you think about it, it's the dripping that gives the gravy a great meaty flavour and not the stock, the flour or the onion. You see, dripping is more than just a fat to cook in; real dripping also has the essence of meat. It's that essence of meat that gives it such depth of flavour and that's why every serious cook should always have dripping to hand.

Years ago dripping would have been found in every kitchen up and down the land. In my own lifetime I have vivid memories of people in the shop asking for fat to make dripping at home. I remember households where the dripping sat in a vessel on a shelf and it was the 'go to' fat for frying, basting and for making Yorkshire puddings. It was also used for deep-frying chips and battered fish. For those of us in the 40+ bracket, we might sometimes linger on the thought that the traditional fry-up or fish and chips today doesn't taste quite the same as it did when we were kids. While many would tell us we were just full of sentimental nostalgia, I can tell you that it has probably got to do with the fat the food is cooked in.

In our wisdom, my generation traded the wonderful flavourful dripping for commercially produced oils and shop bought fats. Quicker and more convenient perhaps, but without even going into the health merits (or demerits as is the case), we have been seriously short changed in the area of taste. Our growing love of cooking with oil (and not olive oil which is the exception) has meant our children have become adults without any knowledge of a dripping taste experience. They've been truly robbed.

Recently at James Whelan Butchers we were getting more and more requests for dripping as people began to slowly cotton on to the wisdom of our grandparents. While they wanted to use dripping, there is a case that a time-poor society can't make it themselves. While dripping is the drips of fat that comes off meat when you cook it, there is another stage in the process before you can reuse it and have proper beef dripping that will last. You must leave it to cool and form two distinct layers. The first layer will be the white fat and the underneath layer will be a jelly like consistency. The jelly is fantastic, used pretty quickly in stews, casseroles or sauces, but it is the white fat that needs to be taken off and clarified. Clarifying is a simple process but it is time consuming and a little messy. Basically, you melt the fat slowly again once you have removed it from the jelly. When it has liquefied, strain it into a bowl or vessel and allow it to set. We usually strain it through muslin for the best results. Dripping is particularly good for browning beef of any kind as you are adding another layer of deep flavour to the already beefy taste.

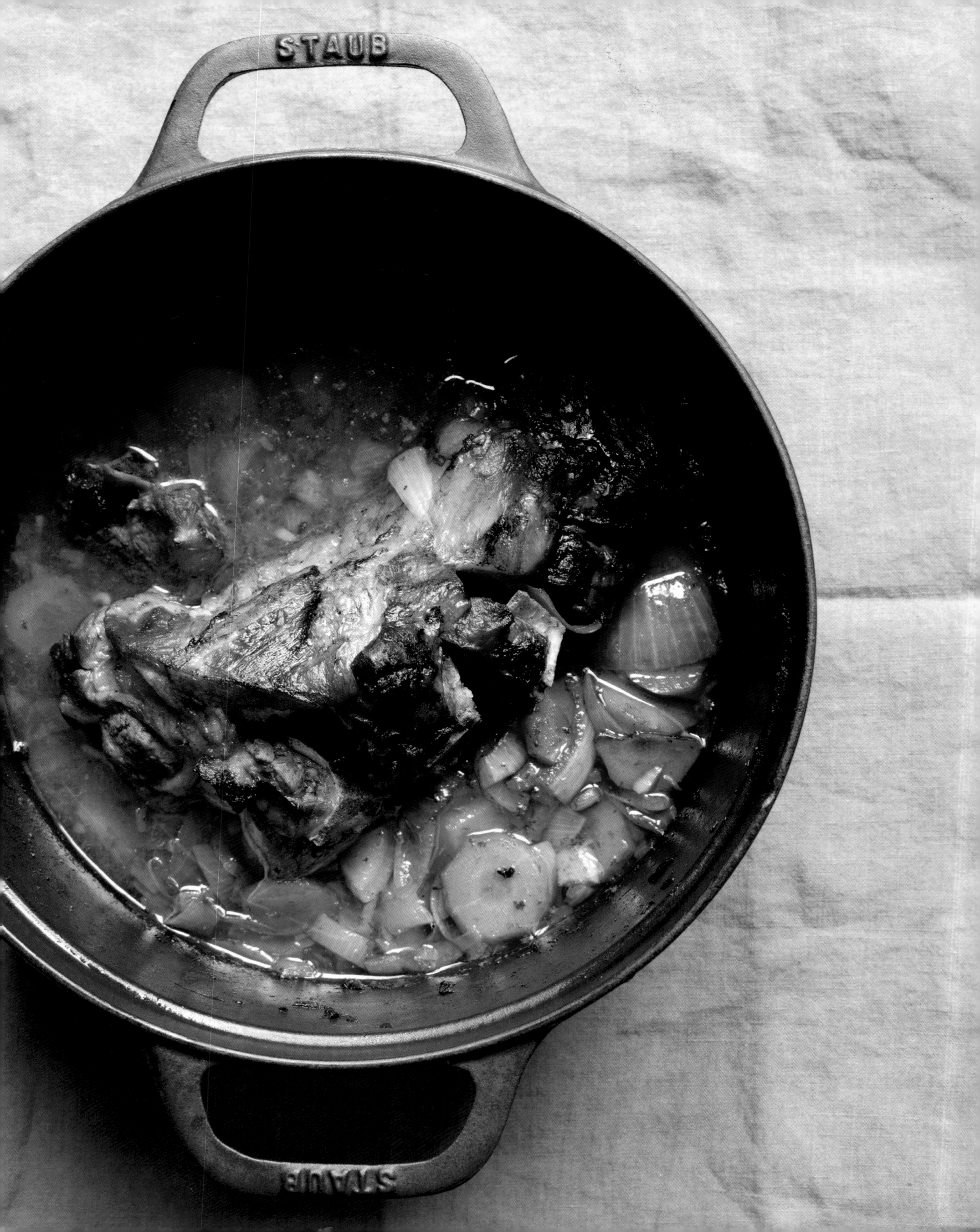
STAUB

MUTTON POT ROAST WITH ONIONS AND CARROTS

It's not that easy to find mutton or hogget in Ireland these days, as modern taste has, for years, preferred the sweeter, more delicate meat of lambs butchered before the connective tissue has time to grow.
In the old times, the greatest asset of sheep was their wool, not their meat, but now it is rare to find ram meat over six months old. When you do come across mature sheep meat, it's best to cook it long and slow.

Mutton, after kid, would have been the meat traditionally found in Irish stew, and this is a pot roast version of it, with a little extra luxury in the form of carrots. A leg of mutton is best poached for a couple of hours, like ham, and served with Colcannon and caper sauce.

Irish lamb is famously delicious, and enjoyed all over the world, but the Calvey's family Achill Mountain Lamb is truly special. Look out for it!

For 4
5 minutes preparation
2 to 3 hours cooking

30 g butter
2 kg piece of neck of mutton
2 large onions
4 carrots
Salt and pepper

Peel and slice the carrots and onions.

Pre-heat the oven to 150 °C.

Heat the butter in a heavy based casserole dish (with a lid) and brown the mutton all over.
Add the carrots and onions and brown them in the mutton fat.

Pour in a glass of water — just so the base of the meat and the vegetables are covered — season lightly with salt and pepper and bring to the boil on the hob.

Once simmering, put the lid on and cook in the oven for 2½ to 3 hours, until the meat is melting.

You can remove some of the fat, before serving with fluffy potato mash.

Belfast city hall on an autumn evening.

HAY SMOKED DUCK AND PITHIVIER, BY ROBBIE KRAWCZYK

For 2
60 minutes preparation
80 minutes cooking

For the duck
1 whole duck
50 g duck fat
1 bay leaf
1 clove garlic
Sprig of rosemary and thyme
Pinch of salt
2 g pepper
3 g coriander seeds
1 litre cold water
50 g salt
30 g sugar

For the jus
10 ml oil
1 onion
1 bulb garlic
½ bottle red wine
Sprig of thyme
Salt and pepper

For the pithivier
Splash of sherry vinegar
2 confit duck legs
1 small shallot
Puff pastry
1 tsp capers
2 tsp chopped flat-leaf parsley
Duck jus (as below)
1 beaten egg for glazing

For the beetroot espuma
1 kg beetroots
60 g hot espuma
1 orange
1 lemon
1 bay leaf
1 sprig rosemary and thyme
20 ml distilled vinegar
Salt and pepper

Day 1, remove both legs and breasts. Place the carcass on an oven tray and roast until golden.
Whilst the carcass is roasting, mix the salt, water and sugar together. Place the duck breasts in a bowl and cover with the brine mix leaving for 8 hours in the refrigerator. Remove and set aside for Day 2.

Place the duck legs along with all the other ingredients into a large vacuum bag and seal on full. Cook in an immersion circulator at 86 °C for 10 hours. Chill and set aside for Day 2.

For the jus, place the roasted bones in a pot and cover in water. Bring to the boil and allow to simmer for 6 hours. Pass through a sieve and refrigerate overnight.

For the Pithivier (Day 2) : pick the meat from the duck legs and place in a pot, along with the finely sliced shallot, capers and flat-leaf parsley. Add some jus to the mix with a splash of sherry vinegar. Roll out some of the puff pastry and, using a circle cutter, cut two circles the same size. Place a small ball of duck in the centre of one. Brush some egg wash around the sides and cover with the second pastry circle. Brush some egg wash over the top and set aside.

Take the stock from the fridge and remove any fat settled on the top.

Peel and cut the onion in quarters, and cut the garlic bulb in half. Heat up a pan with the oil, thyme, salt, pepper, onion and garlic, and when the onion and garlic are browned add the wine. Reduce until sticky. Gradually add all the stock and allow to reduce by about 60%.

Place all ingredients, except the hot espuma, in a pot big enough to hold the beetroot and cover in water. Cook until soft. When cool, peel off the skin and blitz in the Thermomix® at 80 °C until you have a smooth puree. Remove 100 g of puree and reserve. Continue to blend the remaining puree on slow speed, adding a small bit of olive oil and a splash of sherry vinegar. Season and add 30 g of hot espuma to 400 g of puree. Blend and place in a siphon with two shots. Keep warm at around 60 °C.

To complete the dish, place the duck breasts in a vacuum pouch and place in the immersion circulator at 61,5 °C for 25 minutes and allow to rest for 10 minutes in the vacuum pouch. The beetroot espuma can be kept warm in the same immersion circulator.

Place the Pithivier in the oven at 180 °C for 20 minutes.

Heat a small bit of remaining beetroot puree. Heat up a pan and remove the duck from the vacuum bag.

Fry skin side down until crispy. Using a wooden wine box with a sliding lid, lay the duck and cover with hay. Light the hay with a blowtorch and close the box to smother the fire. Leave for 3 minutes. This will create the hay smoke effect.

To present the dish, place a line of puree on the plate. Slice the duck and lay upon the puree. Lay the Pithivier alongside the sliced duck and add the espuma. Dress the dish with 3-4 blackberries around the plate.

IRISH STEW

People, I find, can become a little tetchy over Irish stew recipes. The purists, backed up by authorities on Irish food, swear by a thick, stirred up stew of mutton, onions, floury potatoes, a little thyme and/or parsley, water and nothing else. Even carrots are not meant to get a look in. One thing we do agree on is how much better the dish tastes when reheated the day after cooking.

When I published my grandmother's recipe (moderately thick consistency, waxy potatoes, lamb neck, no carrots) in France in 2005, an angry French blogger declared it as an example of what not to do, and proceeded to add garlic, rosemary and peas to hers, declaring: "At last, an Irish stew worthy of its name".

But you see, whereas some national dishes such as tatin, tiramisu or lasagne can take a good tweak, messing with our stew denatures it because it is its very austerity which makes it authentic. There is little to beat the delicate cooking juices produced by lamb, onions, thyme and potato. It was, and is, a celebration of how very little can taste so good and sustain so well.

I love my grandmother's stew for other reasons than simple taste, of course. It was hers, it is a part of happy childhood memories and, to a certain extent, it doesn't really matter if it is better or worse for its waxy potatoes and extra liquid. As for successful tweaks, taste-wise, there is nothing terribly wrong with adding celery, carrots, turnips or parsnips to the stew's potatoes and onions. The lamb used can be neck or shoulder, or of course the original mutton if you can find it. I do like Nigella Lawson's addition of barley, but really we are moving into entirely new waters — almost, but not quite, as alien as those French peas and garlic.

I'm giving you, then, my grandmother's recipe (cooked in the oven) and also Irish chef Richard Corrigan's (on the hob), for he manages to sublimate and intensify the taste of this dish without straying too far from the original blueprint. Perhaps it's a knack only Irish people are allowed to have.

For 6
2½ hours preparation
40 minutes cooking

3 middle necks of lamb (about 1.8 kg) filleted and boned to make about 1 kg
650 g floury potatoes – Maris Piper, King Edward
650 g waxy potatoes – Desiree or Pentland Javelin
1 kg carrots
2 onions
1 teaspoon fresh thyme leaves
Chopped chives and parsley for garnish
Stock
Bones from the lamb
1 large carrot, quartered
1 onion, quartered
½ stick of celery, quartered
1 bay leaf
2 large sprigs of time
A generous sprig of parsley
6 black peppercorns, lightly crushed

Make the stock. Put the lamb bones in a large, heavy-based saucepan with the vegetables, pepper and salt. Pour in 3 litres of water, bring to the boil and simmer uncovered for 2 hours.

Strain the stock through a fine sieve to remove bones and vegetables, then return it all to the pan. Boil until reduced to about 1.3 litres. You can do all this in the days before and keep it in a covered container in the fridge.

(continued)

Make the stew, cut the lamb into large chunks. Peel the potatoes (keeping both types separate) and cut them into similar sizes to the meat. Put the two different types into separate bowls of cold water to keep them white. Peel the carrots and cut into slightly smaller pieces. Slice the onions into thick rings.

Put the lamb into a large, clean saucepan. Pour in the stock and bring to the boil, skimming off impurities from the surface. Reduce the heat, cover and simmer gently for 10 minutes.

Add the floury potatoes, carrots and onions. Season generously and simmer for a further 10 minutes, stirring occasionally. Add the waxy potatoes and the thyme. Simmer until the lamb is tender (15 to 20 minutes).

Take off the heat, cover (don't stir) and leave for 15 minutes. Garnish and serve.

MY GRANDMOTHER'S IRISH STEW

For 6
10 minutes preparation
2 hours cooking

750 g lamb neck chops
2 onions sliced into rings
500 g waxy potatoes peeled, sliced
Sprig of flat-leaf parsley
Sprig of fresh thyme
Salt and pepper

Pre-heat the oven to 180 °C.

Place alternating layers of potatoes, onions and lamb, starting with the potatoes, and sprinkling a little thyme as you go, in a heavy bottomed casserole dish, seasoning very lightly with salt and pepper.

Top the stew with a layer of potatoes. Pour in 300 ml of water. Cover and cook for 2 hours without stirring.

Leave to rest for 10 or 15 minutes before serving.

BROUGHGAMMON FARM, BALLYCASTLE, CO. ANTRIM

High above the pretty seaside town of Ballycastle, in rolling yet stark countryside, sits Broughgammon Farm, home to Charlie and Sandy Cole, whose parents have farmed Broughgammon since 2004, and whose family have been involved in agriculture in the area since the late 1800s.

These days, Broughgammon is a very different outfit to the usual sheep and beef farms of the area. Young farmers Charlie and Sandy wanted to transform the self-sufficient mixed use farm into a thriving, sustainable, commercial business, and decided to start producing cabrito (young goat meat), rose veal and dried seaweed.

Bucklings, baby male goats, otherwise destined to be put down at birth, are collected from goat dairy farms in Northern Ireland and reared at Broughgammon until they are five months old. They are then butchered in the farm's facility and sold direct from the farm shop or at farmers' markets around the country. Cabrito is a flavoursome and tender meat, tasting slightly like lamb, only without the fat content.

Apart from selling cuts of meat for roasting, casseroles and curries, Charlie and Sandy have developed a range of kebabs, burgers, bacon and fajitas, all going down a treat in Ireland as curious food lovers rediscover this forgotten meat.

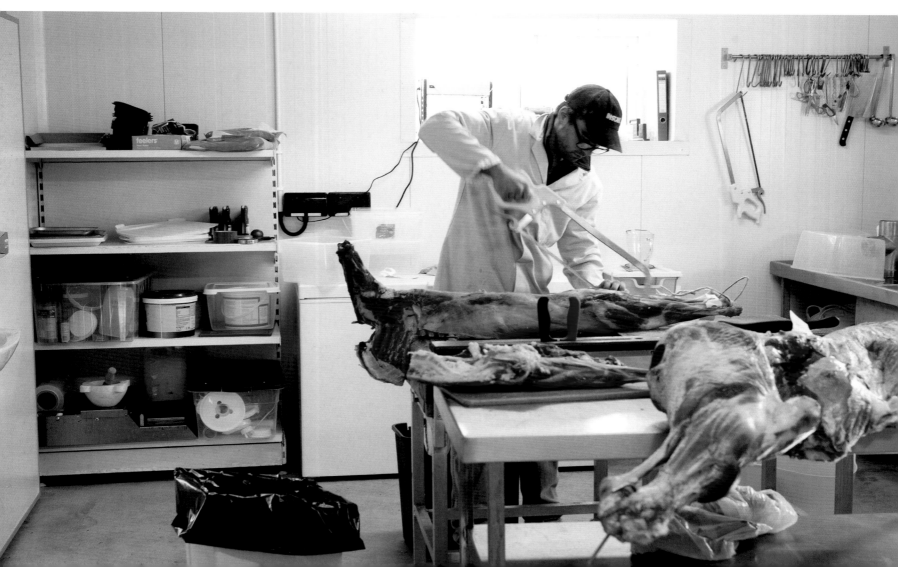

Top left: the Broughgammon ram 'Mr Sexy'. Centre: Becky, Charlie and Sandy Cole. Bottom left: Sandy butchering goat in the farm's facility.

BROUGHGAMMON ROAST CABRITO LEG

Goat has the reputation of being a tough meat, but the younger the animal the more tender it is, and smaller cuts of Broughgammon's cabrito can stand up to the same type of short roasting at high temperatures as beef or lamb. That said, a whole leg cooked on the bone will benefit from a little extra help in the oven as it roasts, and in this recipe I cover the meat during roasting and add a few bits and pieces to the pan.

For 8
2 hours cooking

1 leg of goat
1 clove of garlic
2 or 3 bay leaves
Salt and pepper

Pre-heat the oven to 200 °C.
Rub the goat all over with the garlic, season with salt and pepper and pop it into a roasting tin with the bay leaves.
Let the meat brown for a good 20 minutes or so, turning it a couple of times.
Once browned, cover the goat with foil, trying to keep it snug inside its pan, but without making a hermetic seal. Lower the temperature to 180 °C and roast for 1½ to 2 hours or so with the foil in place.
Remove from the oven and leave to rest before carving and serve with the sauce, the parsnips and the cooking juices from the pan.

JUNIPER, CLOVE AND ONION BREAD SAUCE

This creamy, aromatic sauce goes very well with the gamey taste of cabrito. Add nutmeg or mace to make it even more spicy and flavourful.

For 6 or so
5 minutes preparation
15 minutes cooking
30 minutes resting

500 ml milk
1 onion
1 bay leaf
5 or 6 cloves
5 or 6 juniper berries
4 or 5 slices stale white bread
Salt and pepper

Simmer the milk with the onion studded with cloves, the bay leaf and juniper berries for about 10 minutes.

Make breadcrumbs with the bread and soak them in the milk. Bring to a slow simmer for about 3 minutes then leave to cool and infuse for about 30 minutes.

Remove the onion and the bay leaf, season and serve warm or cold.

ROAST PARSNIPS
AND POTATOES
WITH WHITE SAUSAGE
AND LEMON

This is a rather lovely and slightly luxurious way to accompany bacon or, in this case, cabrito. It's easy to prepare and looks pretty good in all its caramelized, gooey glory, served straight from the roasting tin.

For 6
5 minutes preparation
45 minutes cooking

6 parsnips, peeled and cut lengthways
6 large potatoes, peeled and cut into chunks
2 lemons
1 white pudding, sliced
50 g butter
2 or 3 tablespoons vegetable oil
Salt and pepper

Parboil the vegetables for 10 minutes or so.

Pre-heat the oven to 180 °C

Toss the vegetables with the pudding, the butter and the oil in the roasting pan, then cut up the lemon, squeeze the juice over the pan and leave the pieces to roast alongside the other ingredients.

Put into the oven and roast for about 30 minutes. Keep an eye on it, and stir a couple of times to make sure it cooks evenly, but not too much or you will break up the pieces of pudding.

Season with salt and pepper and serve with the roast meat.

Virginia creeper on Donald Alexander's
Holestone Farm, near Doagh, Co. Antrim.

KEVIN AHERNE

I first bumped into Kevin Aherne at Midleton farmers' market, an Irish food producers' walking, talking, (eating, drinking) hall of fame, where the very best of Irish food is on show and on sale to some of Ireland's most willing customers. Kevin was gathering produce for Sage, his Midleton main street restaurant, and Sage's "twelve mile" menu, created from sustainably produced ingredients all sourced within a twelve mile radius of Midleton.

In creating the menu, Kevin wanted to explore what local really meant, to give himself a "defining line" he would not cross, and to ensure the traceability of the ingredients arriving in his kitchens. The twelve mile limit ensures freshness and a quick turnaround of the food, as many deliveries are made daily and transport times kept to a minimum.

Since opening, Kevin has become very close to his suppliers, creating an almost symbiotic relationship between the restaurant and some of the local producers. Local ingredients featuring on the menu include Noreen and Martin Conroy's Woodside Farm Free Range Pork, Mike Kenneally's Angus beef, Tom Clancy's Ballycotton Free Range Poultry and Ballyhoura Mushrooms.

BEEF CARPACCIO, BLACK PUDDING, CRACKLING AND ONION FOR TWO, BY KEVIN AHERNE

This for me is a great representation of two great products we have in Ireland: beef and pork.

For this dish, the beef I have used is grass-fed Aberdeen Angus. For the pork, I have used a free range saddleback pig. Due to the climate here in Ireland, we produce great grass and vegetables which we use for feed for our livestock. It's one of the reasons they taste so good!

We make our own pudding here at the restaurant for this dish, but for the home cook there are plenty of great puddings available out there. This is a simple dish to cook, technical-wise. Just be sure to use the best of ingredients and let them sing for themselves.

For 2
60 minutes preparation
45 minutes cooking

240 g fillet steak in one piece
80 g black pudding cut into 2 pieces
2 shallots sliced lengthways very finely
100 g pork skin cut into pieces 1 cm x 4 cm
20 g parsley roughly picked not chopped
A fist full of nice crisp lettuce leaves
Salt and pepper for seasoning

Freeze the beef overnight (this might seem odd but it makes it much easier for slicing), remove from the freezer, leave to thaw for 20 minutes then slice as thinly as possible with a straight edged knife. Assemble on 2 plates as shown in picture. Set aside and leave to fully thaw, which will take no more than 1 hour.

While your beef is thawing, simmer the pork skin in boiling water for 20 minutes, then remove from the water and place on a cloth. Dry the skin thoroughly.

Preheat the oven to gas mark 6 place the pork skin and shallots on a baking tray, season with a little salt and pepper and bake for 12 minutes. Remove the onions. Then add the slices of black pudding and bake for a further 12 minutes. Remove from the oven and pat dry any excess grease. Make sure your plates are free from any blood from the Carpaccio. Place 1 piece of pudding on each plate with the pork skin. Garnish with the crispy leaves, onion and parsley then finish with a little seasoning of salt and pepper. Enjoy!

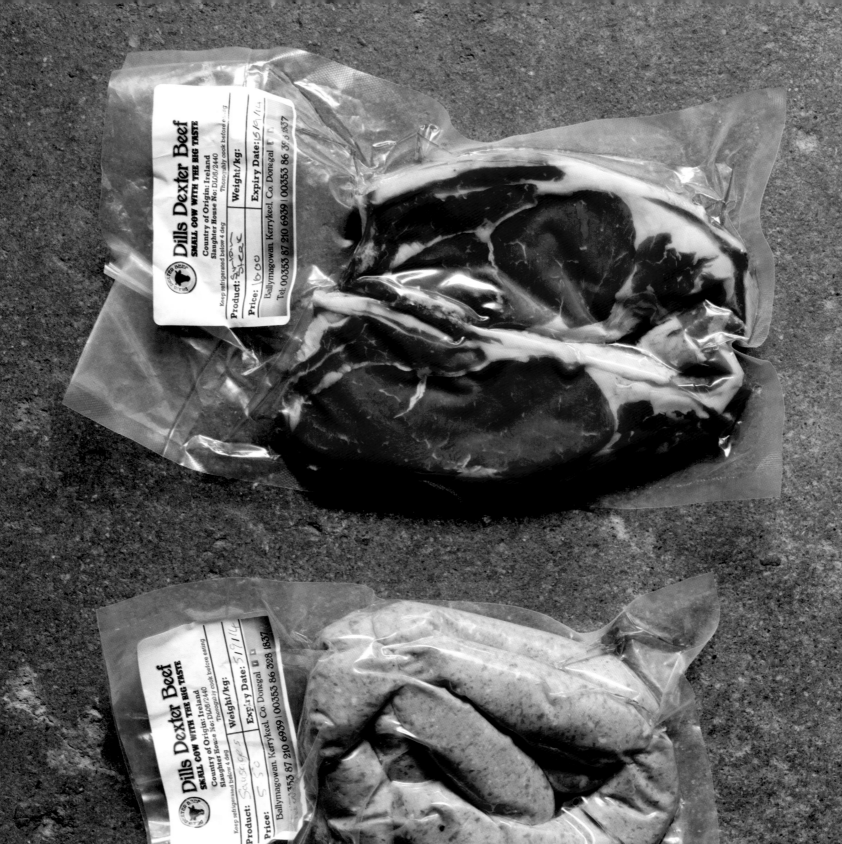

DEXTER BEEF
SAUSAGE ROLLS

Dexter cattle are a native Irish breed, becoming less and less rare thanks to breeder butchers like Sam and Cathy Dill, who have been farming Dexters on Donegal's Fanad pensinsula since 2009. Their first calf was born in 2010; they now have a herd of 160 and have opened their own shop in Letterkenny.

Dexter cattle had all but died out in Ireland, due to the massive influx of big breeds like Charolais and Simmentals, whose size and lean meat make them more profitable and marketable to an increasingly fat-phobic public.

Despite being primarily a dairy breed originally, Dexter meat is very tasty. The cattle are small, with delicate legs and a thick winter coat, allowing them to winter well on scrubbier Irish terrain.

I first tasted Dexter beef sausages bought from Sam Dill at Donal Doherty's Farmers' Market in Bridgend, Donegal. Fruity, firm and, well, beefy, they transported me back to the best I had eaten as a child, often made from the cattle I had seen reared on our farm.

To be honest, I would like you to try these (or a Dexter T bone) simply fried with some good boiled potatoes, but I feel obliged to give you a recipe. Here's the next best thing to eating them whole, I think. A homemade sausage roll.

For about 20 small sausage rolls
20 minutes preparation
30 minutes resting the pastry
25 minutes cooking

250 g plain flour
175 g cold salted butter
1 egg beaten with some water
750 g sausage meat (extracted from the sausages)

Sift the flour into a mixing bowl.

Cut the butter into small chunks and stir into the flour with a knife.

Work the butter into the flour quickly with your fingers, until it resembles a rough crumble.

Add very cold water (a tablespoon to start with) and bring the pastry together until it feels supple but not sticky.

Form it into a ball, wrap in cling film and let it rest in the fridge for at least 30 minutes.

Pre-heat the oven to 220 °C.

Roll the pastry out on a cool, floured surface to about ½ cm thickness and cut into 3 strips about 4 cm wide.

Reform the sausage meat into a sausage shape and set it on the pastry, slightly to one side. Brush the edge of the pastry with the egg, roll the pastry over the meat and press it down to seal the side. You can press the edge with a fork to make a pattern if you like.

Repeat with the rest of the pastry. Brush the tops with the rest of the egg mixture, cut into 2 or 3 cm lengths (or longer, it's up to you) and set them on a lined baking sheet.

Cook for 25 minutes, until golden. Let them cool slightly before serving.

APPLES,
RHUBARB,
DAMSONS
AND BERRIES

Irish fruit preserves and cordials.

SOUR APPLE AND KALE SOUP WITH SWEET APPLE RELISH

Big, ugly, green cooking apples remind me of days spent baking tarts when I was a child and I love using them when I return to Ireland. Like the soft French cookers, Boskoops, they are great in tarts and crumbles. Here, it's their lip-puckering tartness I'm after in this bracing autumn-to-winter soup. The sweet apple relish provides a little contrast to the sharpness. Add cream and butter at will, though the potato and apple should make the soup feel creamy as it is.

For 6 to 8
5 minutes preparation
25 minutes cooking

About 300 g Kale (large bunch)
1 large onion
1 medium potato (100 g about)
Knob of butter
1 tablespoon oil
1 large cooking apple or 2 medium (about 250 g)
500 ml chicken or vegetable stock
Salt and pepper
3 sweet eating apples (Discovery, Tipperary Pippin, Elstar)
1 tablespoon cider vinegar (Wildwood thyme vinegar is lovely here)
Pinch of sugar
Pinch of thyme (optional)

Peel and cube the potato.

Peel and chop the onion.

Wash the kale and remove the toughest part of the stem. Chop roughly.

Heat the butter with the oil in a largish saucepan and sweat the onions with the potatoes.

Warm the stock in a smaller pan.

Throw the kale into the pot and stir from time to time, being careful the kale doesn't stick to the bottom of the pan until it wilts in the steam produced. Pour in the hot stock, give it all a good stir, lower the heat and cook for about 10 minutes.

Peel and core the apple and cut it into chunks. Add to the saucepan and stir it all again. Cook for a further 5 to 10 minutes, until the apple is soft.

Transfer the soup to a blender, or use a handheld blender directly in the pot, and puree until it is fine. Season with salt and pepper and reserve.

Core the sweet apples (leave the skins on for bite and colour) and chop them very finely. Mix through the vinegar with the pinch of sugar and thyme if you have it.

Pour the soup into bowls, top with a spoonful of apple relish and serve with good bread and butter.

IRISH APPLE TART

Every family has their own version of this eternal favourite, that and the apple cake on page 232.
This one is as simple as can be, even if it might take a while to perfect your pastry technique to my mother's
or grandmother's standards. I am not quite there yet.

Just remember that for a truly Irish shortcrust tart, the pastry is always made with a mix of fats and cold
water, never with eggs, and there are usually a couple of cloves added. I like Bramleys in my pie,
but Granny Smiths will do very well also.

For 6 to 8
10 minutes preparation
30 minutes baking

400 g plain flour
100 g lard
100 g salted butter
3 or 4 tablespoons cold water
1 kg cooking apples
2 or 3 cloves
3 tablespoons brown sugar
3 tablespoons milk

Sieve the flour into a large baking bowl.

Cut the fat into chunks and mix it into the flour with a knife, cutting it more finely, before using
your fingers to rub it through.

When the mixture resembles fine breadcrumbs, start mixing in a little water, again with the knife,
then bring the pastry together with your hands.

Do this gradually, since you never know exactly how much water the flour will absorb. It's important not to
make the pastry too sticky, or it will be hard and brittle once cooked, or too dry, as it will crumble too much.

Work the pastry quickly, until it feels supple. Flatten it, cut into two halves, cover them with cling film
and leave to rest in the fridge for at least 30 minutes.

Pre-heat the oven to 180 °C.

Peel, core and slice the apples.

Take the pastry from the fridge and roll it out into two circles.

Press one into the bottom of a deep pie dish, letting the edges fall slightly over the sides.

Fill the pie with the apples, sprinkle them with sugar and tuck the cloves into the fruit.

Cover the apples with the other circle of pastry. Seal the top half to the bottom along the edges
with a little milk and flute them if you like.

Brush the top with milk, make a few pricks with a fork to let the steam out as the apples cook,
and bake in the oven for about 30 minutes until the pastry turns golden.

Sprinkle with caster sugar. Serve with custard or fresh cream.

Coastal walking path near Ballintoy harbour, Co. Antrim.

ROASTED RHUBARB WITH BROWN BREAD CRUMBS, MACE AND BUTTERMILK

A quick and easy dessert using very familiar ingredients in slightly different ways. Buttermilk makes a great tart sauce with poached fruit as an alternative to blander cream or custard. And crisping up treacly soda bread crumbs with a turn in the pan is a good way to use up heels and leftovers. You can freeze what you don't use this time around.

Apples and plums, or a mixture of all three, work just as well here. And you can leave out the mace or replace it with another spice or a mix of spices. Roasting rhubarb this way, rather than stewing the bejaysus out of it, lets it keep a bit of bite.

For 4
5 minutes preparation
25 minutes cooking

450 g rhubarb
50 g sugar
A couple of slices/bits of soda bread, enough for 4 tablespoons of crumbs
1 tablespoon dark brown sugar
50 g butter
Good pinch of ground mace
4 tablespoons buttermilk

Pre-heat the oven to 200 °C. Rinse the rhubarb and drain any water left on it.

Trim the ends and any blemishes, and cut the stalks into equal batons.

Put the rhubarb into an ovenproof dish, sprinkle with the sugar and cover the top with foil (don't let it touch the rhubarb).

Bake for 15 minutes, then remove the foil, spoon the juices over the fruit and give it another 10 minutes or so. The rhubarb should be soft but still holding its shape.

Leave to cool slightly.

As the fruit is baking, heat the butter in the pan and crumble the bread in. Sprinkle with the brown sugar and the mace and let it toast and caramelise for a few minutes, stirring from time to time, until it is crunchy all over.

Leave to cool slightly before serving, sprinkled over the rhubarb with a dash of cold buttermilk.

ROSE COTTAGE SMASHED LOGANBERRY AND BLUEBERRY SALAD

The Mahon Point farmers' market is held in a rather incongruous spot, on the forecourt of a massive, modern shopping centre outside Cork, in stark contrast with ye olde worlde atmosphere of Cork city centre's beautiful English Market. But the food here is fabulous, perhaps even more so than in the English Market, and certainly on a par with the most famous of all Irish farmers' markets, Midleton, where the Irish food revival started.

For 4
10 minutes preparation

4 good handfuls of fresh leaves
100 g blueberries
100 g loganberries
A handful of hazelnuts, crushed
200 g goats cheese
2 tablespoons rapeseed oil
1 tablespoon Wildwood elderflower vinegar

Shake the oil up with the vinegar and dress the leaves. Rinse the fruit quickly. Mash the loganberries slightly with a fork.

Place the leaves on a plate with a few chunks or slices of cheese. Dot the blueberries and loganberries around, sprinkle the hazelnuts and serve.

LOGANBERRY AND RASPBERRY JAM

If you are new to jam-making, this one is for you. It requires no peeling, stoning or hulling, and has only two ingredients with the same weight of sugar to fruit so is very easy to scale up or down until you feel completely confident. Loganberries have the same high level of pectin as raspberries so feel free to mix and match.

For 3 or 4 pots
10 minutes preparation
10 to 15 minutes cooking

1 kg sugar, warmed
1 kg raspberries and loganberries

Put the fruit into a heavy based stainless steel saucepan and heat gently, mashing the fruit gently until the juices run out. Add the sugar, stirring from time to time until you have a thick, pulpy liquid and all the sugar has dissolved. Place a few white plates into the freezer or fridge in readiness for testing the jam.

Increase the heat and bring the jam to a lively boil for about 5 minutes. Remove the scum which will form on top with a slotted spoon as the jam boils.

Test the jam by putting a small blob onto a chilled plate. If little ridges form when you push it with the end of your finger, it is ready. Remove from the heat and let the jam settle before pouring it into spanking clean jamjars. I always seal with screw-on lids and turn the jars upside down as they cool.

HIGH SUMMER SALAD WITH BALLYWALTER STRAWBERRIES

This is more of a tease than an introduction, as your chances of tasting exquisite Ballywalter Estate late strawberries, picked straight off the plant, in late October, as I did, are pretty slim.
I was lucky enough to have them handed to me by the lady of the house herself, and here I wanted to celebrate the occasion, and the taste! I guess it's also a way of saying that not all the consequences of global warming are terrible, even if these intensely sweet and pungent fruits are little solace, set against the damage being done to our planet. *"Il n'y a plus de saisons"* the old folk like to lament in France. October strawberries in County Down would certainly prove them right.

The image shows an altogether more comforting plate, with in-season baby rocket and nasturtium flowers wich are easily found (or grown!). Teamed with firm, juicy strawberries, brought alive by gorgeous, floral Wildwood vinegars from Connemara, it makes a lovely summer starter or side salad.

For 4
5 minutes preparation

4 good handfuls of baby rocket leaves
8 or 10 nasturtium flowers
A dozen or so strawberries
2 tablespoons rapeseed oil
1 tablespoon Wildwood Wild Mountain Thyme and Organic Honey vinegar

Mix the vinegar with the oil. Slice the strawberries and toss all the ingredients together. Serve at once.

QUICK PICKLED STRAWBERRIES

These are quite delicious, and a good way of prolonging the season even more.

For 1 large jar
10 minutes preparation
3 minutes cooking
1 night resting

300 g of strawberries, washed, hulled and cut in half
80 ml white wine vinegar
1 heaped teaspoon sugar
1 heaped teaspoon fine salt
2 Cracked black peppercorns

Bring the vinegar, salt sugar and 80 ml water to a boil, stirring to dissolve the sugar and salt. Pour the hot brine over the sliced strawberries and stir gently.

Let them rest and cool before covering and putting them in the fridge overnight.

They will keep in the fridge for a good week or 10 days.

OX, BELFAST

OX restaurant, Belfast exploded onto Ireland's food scene only a few years ago. Their wildly creative cooking, using stunning local produce, as well as the high ceilings and laid back atmosphere of this former tile shop, instantly raised the bar, both for the island as a whole, and for Belfast, which had been struggling to assert itself as a city with a decent modern food scene.

Now that scene is well and truly established, and OX's manager, Alain Kerloc'h, and chef Stevie Toman have opened the very beautiful wine bar and restaurant overflow, OX Cave, right next door, while sous-chef Gareth McCaughey is about to open his own place in Belfast's Cathedral Quarter. It's a tight team, with young pastry chef Ciara McGhee driving the dessert station under Alain and Stevie's watchful eye. Alain Kerloc'h brings his impeccable taste and insatiable curiosity to the wine list, along with perhaps the best casual dining service in Ireland, honed by his years with Alain Passard in Paris and then Mauro Colagreco in Menton. The décor, like Harry's Shack in Portstewart, is by Belfast duo Oscar and Oscar, who carefully source pieces made from beautiful native timber (OX Cave's bar is carved from a slice of tree trunk with bark intact), many of them from old Irish buildings, schools and convents, giving their spaces a unique, yet warmly familiar patina.

OX pastry chef Ciara McGhee with owner manager Alain Kerloc'h. Top centre: Stevie Toman at the pass.

APPLE AND CLOVE JELLY

The crab apple jelly, gently scented with cloves and spread on toasted, buttered scones was one of my favourite things when I was a child. The recipe requires a little trial and error, but it is a forgiving one, and a stock of these jars to use over a chilly winter is well worth the effort.

For 3 kg (six pots or so)
30 minutes preparation
Overnight straining
1 hour 15 minutes cooking

3 kg cooking or crab apples
3 litres water
4 or 5 cloves
Sugar (according to amount of apple juice)

Chop the apples up, cores and skins and all, removing only stalks and any bruised parts.

Put them in a large pan with the water and simmer for a good hour, until they have stewed down into a brown pulp.

Strain the pulp overnight through a jelly bag into a non-metallic container. Do not press it or you will make the jelly cloudy.

Measure the juice. For every pint (600 ml) you will need a pound (450 g) of sugar, so get your calculators and converters ready.

Warm the sugar and put it into a pan with the juice. Bring to the boil and boil hard, without stirring, for 10 minutes until you reach setting point. Test the jelly on dishes chilled in the fridge. If it makes little ridges after cooling down when you push with your finger, it is ready. If you use a sugar thermometer, I'm told it should say 105/106 °C.

Skim the surface, pour carefully into clean, dry pots (add a clove to each if you like) and seal.

BAKED APPLES WITH PORTER CAKE CRUMBS AND WHISKEY CUSTARD

Very much in the same spirit as the roasted rhubarb on page 216, here the baked fruit is accompanied by the richest of egg custards. Truly unbeatable when made with thick Irish cream, farmyard eggs and a dash of Bushmills.

Use Bramleys if you like your baked apples very fluffy and tart. Braeburns or any other eating apple will do otherwise.

For 4
10 minutes preparation
30 minutes cooking

4 medium sized Bramley, Braeburn or eating apples
50 g butter
4 teaspoons brown sugar
4 tablespoons porter cake (or dark fruit cake) crumbs
30 g butter
250 ml fresh milk
250 ml single cream
5 egg yolks
100 g sugar
Dash of Bushmills (or another Irish whiskey)

Pre-heat the oven to 180 °C.

Core the apples, sit them upright in an ovenproof dish and put a little butter and a teaspoon of sugar in the gap where the core used to be.

Put them in the oven and bake for about 25 minutes.

Meanwhile, make the custard and the crumbs.

Bring the milk and the cream to the boil in a saucepan but be very careful not to boil them.

Whisk the egg yolks with the sugar until they have doubled in volume and turned white.

Pour the hot milk onto the yolks, whisking as you go. Tip the eggy cream back into the pan and heat again, stirring all the while, until the custard starts to thicken. When the custard coats the back of a spoon, immediately remove the pan from the heat and pour the custard into a cold serving bowl to prevent it from curdling. Add a dash of whiskey.

Heat the butter in a frying pan and fry the crumbs until they are crispy. Let them cool slightly.

Serve the apples in bowls with the hot custard and the crumbs sprinkled over.

Green Gates B&B, Ardara, Co. Donegal.

PLUM AND APPLE TART WITH ALMA'S SHORTCRUST PASTRY

Alma was the mother of Deirdre Rooney (whose wonderful photos make this book beautiful), and like many Irish bakers, did not use only butter in her pastry. My own mother's was made with butter and Stork margarine, back in the days when we were more trusting of those who manufactured our ingredients, and only the result mattered.

Alma favoured half butter, half lard, and it does make for a wonderfully tasty and flaky crust. In Northern Ireland especially, lard still sits proudly on supermarket shelves alongside the butter. Now that it, and other once banished saturated fats are back in favour, why not have a go at this pastry and transform your tarts? The rule of thumb for traditional Irish shortcrust is two parts flour to one part fat, no eggs to bind, only cold water. The quantities here are enough to make a pie with a bottom crust, so simply double them if you want to encase the fruit.

For 8
30 minutes preparation
30 minutes (at least) resting for the pastry
35 minutes cooking

250 g plain flour
75 g cold (not too hard) butter
75 g cold lard
1 tablespoon sugar
2 to 3 tablespoons very cold water
4 or 5 cooking apples (Bramleys)
6 or 8 plums
50 g butter
2 tablespoons sugar

Sieve the flour into a large baking bowl.

Cut the fat into chunks and mix it into the flour with a knife, cutting it more finely, before using your fingers to rub it through.

When the mixture resembles fine breadcrumbs, start mixing in a little water, again with the knife, and bring the pastry together with your hands.

Do this gradually, since you never know exactly how much water the flour will absorb. It's important not to make the pastry too sticky, or it will be hard and brittle once cooked, or too dry, as it will crumble too much.

Work the pastry quickly, until it feels supple. Flatten it into a round, cover with cling film and leave it to rest in the fridge for at least 30 minutes.

Pre-heat the oven to 180 °C.

Roll the pastry out on a floured surface and press it into the base of a 22/24 cm tart tin. Trim the edges and brush them with a little milk to give them a nice colour.

Peel, core and cut up the apples. Halve the plums and remove their stones. Slice further or leave them in halves — it's up to you.

Fill the tart base with the fruit, dot with the butter and sprinkle the sugar over.

Bake for 30 to 40 minutes, until the apples are caramelized and the pastry golden and crisp.

IRISH APPLE CAKE

There are as many versions of this in Ireland as there are shapes of apples, it would seem. As the recipe has been handed down orally, or scribbled on the back of an old shopping list, or in the margin of a cookbook, it has slowly evolved and multiplied, winding its way down the branches of many a family tree.

This one is from Midleton in Cork, where the apple cakes are tall and round. It is dense and crunchy on top, with the odd blackberry making a little pocket of tart juice in the white apple-y sponge.

Sometimes, apple cakes are like Ina Daly's. Ina is from Ballydehob, in West Cork, and bakes hers in a rectangular baking tin, with a layer of apples topped with fluffy sponge. When someone told her I wrote recipes, she said, "Faith? Is it easy to read her writing?".

For 8 to 12
10 minutes preparation
45 to 50 minutes cooking

400 g flour
2 teaspoons baking powder
175 g salted butter, very cold
150 g sugar + 2 tablespoons for the top of the cake
4 cooking apples
150 g blackberries (optional)
2 eggs
175 ml fresh milk
½ teaspoon good vanilla extract

Grease and flour a round, 20 cm springform cake tin. Or use a cake tin liner.

Pre-heat the oven to 180 °C

Sift the flour and baking powder into a very large mixing bowl.

Cut the butter into small cubes and rub it through the flour with your fingers until the mixture looks like breadcrumbs, then stir in the sugar.

Peel, core and chop the apples into 2 cm chunks. Toss them through the flour mixture.

Beat the eggs and milk in a separate bowl and stir in the vanilla extract. Pour the batter into the mixing bowl and mix it in with a wooden spoon or spatula until just combined into a thick dough. Be careful not to work it too much. Add the blackberries now if you are using them.

Tip this dough into the prepared cake tin and smooth the top with the spoon or spatula. Sprinkle the sugar over the top of the cake and bake for 45/50 minutes, until it is well risen and slightly golden and cracked on top. Test the cake with a knife or a skewer, which will come out clean if the cake is baked.

Remove from the oven and leave to cool for 10 minutes or so in the tin before turning out onto a wire rack and leaving to cool completely.

JESS MURPHY

A Kiwi who adopted Ireland and has been adopted right back, JESS MURPHY's boisterous, colourful cooking does that wonderful thing of soothing and energizing you at the same time.

Jess is much loved across Ireland, and her and husband David's restaurant Kai, on the famous Sea Road in Galway City, has become a local institution, with a queue for lunch and brunch way out the door on most days. It's a warm, happy, wood-clad space, with a skylight spilling light onto tables and over a bar covered with some of the most gorgeous cakes in Galway.

Jess's dishes use only the best local produce, organic where possible, and her love and understanding of ingredients shine through in every bite.

She is a big fan of cooking game, stemming from hunting trips when she was back home in New Zealand.

JESS MURPHY'S LEMON AND RASPBERRY MERINGUE PIE

Jess Murphy's New Zealand roots show in her freestyle, wildly original cooking. Her love for Ireland and Ireland's produce has that added intensity of a recent convert. Her radical, generous food champions excellent local producers at her cosy, modern restaurant Kai.

For 4 to 6
5 minutes preparation time
25 cooking preparation time

For the sweet pastry
125 g butter
68 g caster sugar
1 egg
1 yolk
250 g flour
37 g icing sugar
37 g ground almonds

For the lemon curd
5 lemons (juice and zest)
9 yolks
275 g castor sugar
300 g fresh cream
45 g corn flour
100 g butter
200 g fresh raspberries

For the meringue
4 egg whites
250 g sugar
30 g water

Mix the butter and sugar until creamy, scrape the bowl down then add the eggs and the yolk. Mix for 10 seconds then add the flour, icing sugar and ground almonds. Mix a little bit and finish off by hand. Leave it to rest at least 2 hours in the fridge.

Roll the pastry, line a 22 cm tarte case, rest for 15 to 20 minutes in the fridge then cook it blind at 180 °C until it turns a nice colour. Leave it to cool down.

Mix the lemon juice, zest, yolks, sugar, cream and cornflour in a bain-marie at around 85 °C. Don't let the bowl touch the water, leave the mix to cook until it reaches a thick consistency like that of custard. Then add the butter, mix it then put away in a container with cling film on top, and leave to rest in the fridge for 2 hours.

Add the lemon curd to the tarte case with the fresh raspberries.

For the meringue, beat the egg whites with a whisk until foamy. At the same time, put the sugar and water to cook in the pan until the sugar has reached 118 °C. Then pour the syrup into the egg whites, slowly increasing the speed of the mixer. Leave to mix till firm consistency is obtained (the bottom of the bowl should be at room temperature).

Spread the meringue on top and use the blow torch, or the oven at around 220 °C for a few minutes. Leave to cool before serving.

APPLE CRUMBLE
BY DEREK CREAGH,
HARRY'S BRIDGEND

For 4
5 minutes preparation
40 minutes cooking

For the topping
110 g unsalted butter
90 g plain flour
70 g caster sugar
50 g ground almonds
60 g ginger bread
Pinch of salt

For the apple mix
4 Braeburn apples
1 vanilla pod
60 g unsalted butter
40 g sultanas
A little ground cinnamon to taste

For the custard
1 vanilla pod
100 ml whole milk
100 ml double cream
2 egg yolks
50 g caster sugar

Melt the butter and combine the crumble ingredients until reduced to crumbs.

Spread mixture evenly across a baking tray, and bake for up to 25 min at 180 °C until golden brown.

Halve the vanilla pod and scrape out the seeds.

Peel and core the apple, and cut into small cubes.

Melt the butter in a pan and cook the apples for several minutes, then add the cinnamon, vanilla and sultanas and cook for a few minutes more.

Place the mixture in an ovenproof dish, cover with the crumble topping and bake for 10 minutes.

Scrape the seeds from the vanilla pod, and whisk the egg yolks and sugar together until light and creamy. Heat the milk and cream, and add the vanilla seeds until simmering. Pour cream and vanilla mix onto eggs and beat to combine.

Return the mixture to the pan and heat until thickened, stirring constantly.

Remove from the heat, pour into a cooled bowl or jug and leave to cool.

Serve with the apple crumble.

CAKES
AND
BREADS

Irish pan bread.

BLAA WITH BLACK PUDDING, CARAMELIZED ONIONS AND QUINCE PASTE

The Waterford Blaa is a whiter-than-white, doughy bread roll with PGI (Protected Geographical Indication), as its origins can be linked back to the arrival of the French Huguenots in the city in the 1690s. The same traditional recipe has been handed down from generation to generation as in the oral tradition.

But PGI does not bring this ball of bleached flour any real nutritional or taste advantages; its main appeal is its fluffy texture, and how wonderfully that contrasts with a few slices of crisp bacon of a morning. Just like the best croissants in France, Blaas are only available until around lunchtime in Waterford, and are made by a couple of family bakeries who dispatch them around the town. After midday, they start to pucker, dry out and harden. Schools sell them in their tuck shops for elevenses, dusting uniforms and noses with flour as pupils head back into the classroom.

The breakfast roll or bap, as this Belfast-born girl calls it, is a superb way to eat Irish breakfast on the hoof or when you are too sleepy and hungry to be bothered with knives and forks. Here's a rather swanky, fruity alternative to the classic bacon, sausage, egg and ketchup.

For 4
5 minutes preparation
35 minutes cooking

3 onions, peeled and chopped
50 g butter
Salt and pepper
Dash of cider vinegar
4 Blaas
400 g Irish black pudding
30 g butter for frying
100 g good quince paste
Baby rocket or other salad leaves

Start with the onions, as they always take longer than you think.

Melt the butter in a frying pan and sweat the chopped onions. Keep stirring until they soften but do not brown them too soon or they will be bitter. Let them cook in their own juices, mingled with the butter, until they slowly caramelise in their own sugar and lose their astringency. This takes a good 25 minutes, but it is worth it, so be patient.

If really you cannot wait this long, by all means crisp and fry the onions over a higher heat for a shorter time. The flavour will be sharper, and it might drown the quince a little. It's up to you.

When the onions are the way you want them, remove the pan from the heat and reserve.

Slice the black pudding and fry it in the butter until it is crispy.

Butter the blaas (you could toast them, but I wouldn't; it's better to make the most of their pillowy insides), set some leaves on the butter and top with the pudding, the hot onions and some quince paste.

Close the blaa and bite through its softness to the hot crunch beneath. Unbeatable.

HICKEY'S CRUSTY GRINDER CRAB SANDWICHES

Hickey's bakery in Clonmel makes this marvellous soft white bread with a chewy caramelly crust. It is simply perfect with peppery roquette and nasturtium flowers, sweet Irish crab meat and creamy lemon-seaweed mayo, for a seaside picnic or quick summer lunch.

For 4
15 minutes preparation

4 tablespoons mayonnaise
1 tablespoon double cream
1 teaspoon dried seaweed
Zest of half a lemon
200 g crab meat
Salt and pepper
8 slices of Hickey's Crusty Grinder
2 handfuls baby rocket
Nasturtium flowers
30 g butter

Mix the seaweed, lemon zest and cream into the mayonnaise. Add the crab meat, season lightly and mix again. Spread the crab on two slices of bread, set some leaves and a flower or two on top, and close with a second, lightly buttered slice. Cut in two.

HANGOVER BLAA

This also works with any white bread.

For 1
2 minutes preparation

1 fresh blaa
25g butter
A packet of cheese and onion crisps (preferably Tayto)

Slice the blaa, butter both sides, set a good handful of crisps on one half, close with the other and crunch.

GOOD THINGS CAFE NO-KNEAD BREAD, ADAPTED FROM JIM LAHEY, SULLIVAN STREET BAKERY

For 1 bread
1½ hour preparation
14 to 20 hours rising

3 cups of bread flour — plus more for dusting
¼ teaspoon instant yeast
1¼ teaspoons salt
Cornmeal or wheat bran as needed

Stage 1: In a large bowl, combine flour, yeast and salt. Add 1½ cups of water and stir until blended — the dough will be shaggy and sticky. Cover the bowl with cling film and let the dough rest for at least 12 hours — preferably for about 18 hours, at warm room temperature (about 70°C).

Stage 2: (12 to 24 hours later) The dough is ready when its surface is dotted with bubbles. Lightly flour a work surface and place the dough on it. Sprinkle with a little more flour and fold it over on itself once or twice. Cover loosely with cling film and let it rest for about 15 minutes.

Stage 3: Using just enough flour to keep the dough from sticking to the work surface or your fingers, gently and quickly shape into a ball. Generously coat a cotton towel with flour, wheat bran or cornmeal. Put the dough on the towel (seam side down), and dust with more flour, bran or cornmeal. Cover with another cotton towel and let rise for about 2 hours. When it is ready, the dough will be more than double in size
and will not readily spring back when poked with a finger.

Stage 4: At least a ½ hour before the dough is ready, pre-heat the oven to very hot. Put a 6 to 8 quart heavy covered pot (cast iron, enamel, Pyrex or ceramic) into the oven as it heats. When the dough is ready, carefully remove the pot from the oven. Slide your hand under the towel and turn the dough over into the pot, seam side up — it may look a mess but that is OK. Shake the pot once or twice if the dough is unevenly distributed — it will straighten out as it bakes. Cover with the lid and bake for 30 minutes, then remove the lid and bake for another 15 to 30 minutes until the loaf is beautifully browned. Cool on a rack.

IRISH NO YEAST / NO KNEAD SODA BREADS

I think it is my love for this bread, and the inversely proportionate effort involved in producing it, which has forever, it seems, stopped me from joining the growing ranks of homemade white or sourdough bread makers. That and the fact that I have been living in France for the past 25 years with excellent bakeries on my doorstep, and that my ex father-in-law is a flour miller. His absolute respect and admiration for the boulangers he supplied imbued in me a sort of moral obligation to buy their bread. Making my own was considered a bit of a betrayal — that and one fewer customer for him, of course.

I did once have a bash at learning. In Ireland, in fact. But there were too many variables, too many things that could go wrong. There were, and still are, other culinary Everests I would like to climb before entering into the Sacred Fraternity of The Sourdough Starter.

Many of the bread recipes in this book are, therefore, other people's. I fully realize that you may not be quite as lazy and defeatist as me when it comes to making your daily loaf, and would like to tackle yeast and knocking back and kneading with the best of them, so some of Ireland's best bakers and chefs have very kindly contributed to my pages and so to your cooking repertoire.

Elizabeth David said: "Everyone who cooks, in however limited a way, should know how to make a loaf of soda bread". This Irish delicacy — nutty, moist and crumbly — goes so well with so many of Ireland's other famous dishes and is pretty much irresistible on its own, or toasted with Irish butter. It's easy to see that, once again, Elizabeth was right.

DARINA ALLEN'S BROWN BREAD FOR BEGINNERS

Darina Allen is Ireland's most active and effective campaigner for quality Irish food, produced sustainably. Her and her brother Rory's cookery school at Ballymaloe is now world famous, training entire generations of young chefs and sending them out inspired by both the school's ethics and Ireland's culinary heritage. Darina very kindly gave me permission to include her recipe for Irish brown bread, very often the first Irish recipe many budding cooks will try.

For 1 loaf
10 minutes preparation
45 minutes baking

400 g stone-ground wholemeal flour
75 g plain white flour
1 teaspoon of salt
1 level teaspoon bicarbonate of soda (aka bread soda or baking soda)
1 organic egg
1 tablespoon of sunflower or olive oil
1 teaspoon of honey
425 ml of butter milk
2 generous tablespoons of seed mix – I use Good 4 U Sunflower mix, which you can get in loads of supermarkets.

Pre-heat the oven to 200 °C / 180 °C fan / gas mark 6.

Put all the dry ingredients — wholemeal flour, plain flour, bicarbonate of soda and salt — into a large mixing bowl. Mix together lightly with the tips of your fingers.
Mix the buttermilk, egg, honey and oil in another bowl until well blended.

Get a loaf tin (23 x 12.5 x 5 cm) and pour a teaspoon of oil into it. Coat the whole of the inside of the tin with your hands, to prevent the bread from sticking.

Now make a well in the dry ingredients. Pour about a third of the milk mixture into the well. Mix the mixture with your hand until it begins to get sticky. Don't mix it too much though; it will go a bit tough; in the end if you do. Add another third of the milk mixture and mix again. Finally, add the last third and mix.

The dough is supposed to be wet and sticky, so much so that you can pour it into the loaf tin. Pop the filled tin into the oven on the middle shelf for between 45 minutes and one hour. Sprinkle seeds on top, halfway through baking so they do not burn.

Once the bread is nice and brown, take it out of the oven and test the base to hear if it sounds hollow when tapped. If so, leave it to cool completely on a wire rack before cutting.

SWEET, SOFT TREACLE BROWN BREAD

This is really cake pretending to be bread. I suggest you serve it as a course on its own with some homemade butter, or your guests will have no room left for the rest of your cooking.

For 1 loaf
10 minutes preparation
50 minutes cooking

375 g coarse wholemeal flour
75 g wholemeal (or white) flour
75 g rolled oats
1½ teaspoons bicarbonate of soda
1 tablespoon treacle
1 tablespoon runny honey
475 ml buttermilk
A good pinch of salt

Pre-heat the oven to 200 °C.

Sieve the flours and the bicarbonate of soda into a large mixing bowl. Add the oats and stir again.

In a small bowl, mix the honey and the treacle into a little buttermilk to loosen them and make them easier to mix with the flour. Make a well in the centre of the big bowl and pour in the buttermilk and the treacle and honey mixture.

With your hands, bring the dough together. It will be soft and slightly sticky. Do not overwork it, and do not knead it!

Make it into a round and set it on the floured baking sheet. Cut a cross in the top to allow it to rise evenly.

Bake for around 50 minutes, checking it from time to time.

It is cooked when the crust is golden brown and the loaf sounds hollow when you lift and tap it underneath.

Leave it to cool under a damp tea towel.

PLAIN SODA BREAD (WHEATEN BREAD IN NORTHERN IRELAND)

Found everywhere sliced or whole, in round or oblong loaves or in individual farls, wheaten bread is a breakfast and high tea favourite in Northern Ireland and great with smoked salmon or cheese.

For 1 loaf
5 minutes preparation
30 minutes baking

250 g plain flour
250 g wholemeal flour
1 barely rounded teaspoon baking soda
1 teaspoon salt
450 to 475 ml buttermilk

Pre-heat the oven to 225 °C. Mix the flours in a large, wide bowl, add the salt and sieved baking soda. Lift the flour up with your fingers to distribute the salt and baking soda.

Make a well in the centre and pour in all the buttermilk. With your fingers stiff and outstretched, stir in a circular movement from the center to the outside of the bowl in ever increasing concentric circles. When you reach the outside of the bowl, seconds later, the dough should almost have come together. Give it a bit of a quick knead in the bowl to include all the flour.

Sprinkle a little flour on the worktop. Turn the dough out onto the floured worktop.

Sprinkle a little flour on your hands. Gently tidy the dough around the edges and transfer to an oven tray. Tuck the edges underneath with your hand; gently pat the dough with your fingers into a loaf about 4 cm thick. Now wash and dry your hands.

Cut a deep cross into the bread (this is called "blessing the bread") and then prick it in the center of the four sections to let the fairies out of the bread.

Bake in the pre-heated oven for 15 minutes, then turn the oven down to 200 °C for a further 15 minutes. Turn the bread upside down and cook for a further 5 to 10 minutes until done (the bottom should sound hollow when tapped). Cool on a wire rack.

China collection, Nancy's bar, Ardara Co. Donegal.

SODA FARLS

In Northern Ireland, when we say "soda bread" we are usually referring to soda farls, fluffy white bread cooked in a flattened round shape, made with buttermilk on a smooth griddle. Our wheaten bread is what is known as soda bread "down south".

The term farl comes from an Ulster Scots word *fardel*, meaning a fourth or a quarter. The soda is cut into four as it cooks. Nowadays you will find wheaten and treacle soda farls as well as a version with raisins, but nothing as fancy would have been offered back in the day. They are best eaten straight from the griddle, hot with butter and jam or marmalade; and they very often find their way into an Ulster Fry.

For 4
3 minutes preparation
20 minutes cooking

300 g white flour
1¼ teaspoons baking soda
Good pinch of salt
250 ml buttermilk

Pre-heat a flat griddle or a heavy bottomed saucepan.

Mix the flour, salt and baking soda together and make a well in the centre.

Working very quickly (the buttermilk sets the baking soda off immediately), preferably with your hands, mix the buttermilk into the flour to make a soft dough.

Shape the dough into a round of about 1½ cm high and set it into the pan or on the griddle. Mark it across the top to form 4 quarters, without cutting through the dough entirely.

Cook for 20 minutes, turning the soda so that both sides are done and the bread is nicely risen.

For treacle sodas, heat the buttermilk gently, (do not boil or it will split!) add 1 generous tablespoon of black treacle and mix gently to dissolve it. Leave to cool before proceeding with the recipe as above.

To make fruit sodas simply add 50 g raisins or sultanas, or a mix of dried fruits to the dry ingredients and proceed with the recipe.

Wheaten sodas are made just like plain ones, you just replace the flour with wholemeal flour, or use half and half.

TEA BRACK

This is an unyeasted brack (from the Irish *brac* meaning speckled) so denser than the barmbrack and another recipe which is more cake than bread. The traditional yeasted versions are not unlike a French raisin *brioche*, though the tea does give a darker hue.

For 1 loaf
1 night's soaking
5 minutes preparation
1 hour baking

225 g plain flour
110 g sultanas
110 g currants
175 ml strong, hot tea
110 g brown sugar
1 heaped teaspoon baking powder
1 egg, beaten
½ teaspoon mixed spice
A little butter to grease the tin

In a largish mixing bowl, soak the fruit in the hot tea overnight or for at least 4 hours. Pre-heat the oven to 170 °C.

Grease a medium loaf tin. Mix all the ingredients into the soaked fruit and tip them into the tin.

Smooth the mixture and bake in the oven for about 1 hour, checking the cake with a skewer or sharp knife to make sure it is baked through. If the knife comes out clean and the top is nicely golden, remove from the oven and leave to cool for 5 minutes before turning out onto a wire rack until it is just warm and ready to eat.

DERMOT STAUNTON'S GUINNESS BREAD FROM DELAHUNT, DUBLIN

One of Dublin's latest restaurant darlings, a former grocers, mentioned in James Joyce's *Ulysses*, Delahunt is first and foremost a beautiful room. Dermot Staunton's clever, hearty cooking uses only seasonal produce, and even his bread is irresistible. Here's the recipe.

For 1 loaf (medium loaf tin)
10 minutes preparation
50 minutes cooking

300 g wholemeal flour
75 g plain flour
50 g porridge oats
50 g pinhead oats
1½ teaspoon bread soda
½ teaspoon salt
20 g tablespoon brown sugar
20 g butter, diced
200 ml milk
100 ml black treacle
150 g Guinness

Pre-heat an oven to 170 °C.

Sift the plain flour, bread soda and salt into a large bowl. Add the wholemeal flour and mix well. Rub the butter into the flour until it resembles breadcrumbs. Add the porridge oats, pinhead oats and sugar and mix together.

Make a well in the centre and add the wet ingredients. Mix together quickly, trying not to overwork the dough.

Grease and flour a bread tin. Place the dough in the tin to ¾ of the height, no more.

Tap the tin against a work surface.

Make an incision down the centre of the bread the length of the tin. Dust the surface with plain flour and more porridge oats.

Place in the oven for 40 minutes.

Remove the bread from the tin and return to the oven for a further 10 minutes or until a skewer comes out clean.

Allow to cool on a wire rack before slicing.

PETER WARD'S PINT GLASS SODA BREAD FOR HIS SON, JEFF

Every parent worries about their children eating well when they leave home and have to cook for themselves. Peter Ward, one of Ireland's first "good food warriors", founded Country Choice food store and cafe in Nenagh, Co. Tipperary, in 1982, and when his son Jeff (who is dyslexic) left to study in Dublin, Peter thought up this method so Jeff could easily make the soda bread he missed so much from home. After all, the one piece of "equipment" an Irish student is certain to possess in his kitchen is a pint glass.

For 1 loaf
5 minutes preparation
25 minutes cooking

1 pint glass coarse whole meal flour
1 pint glass white baking flour
Enough salt to coat the bottom of a pint glass (1 teaspoon)
Enough baking soda to coat the bottom of a pint glass (1 teaspoon)
1 tablespoon butter, not too hard
¾ pint buttermilk

Pre-heat the oven to 225 °C.

Mix the dry ingredients, then make a well in the centre and add the wet (the buttermilk).

Mix with a light hand (shape it like a claw says Darina Allen) in circular movements, quickly drawing in the flour from the side of the bowl.

Tip the dough out onto a floured surface and shape into a round loaf.

Cut a cross in the centre and cook for 25 minutes, until golden on top and hollow sounding beneath.

OX restaurant, Belfast,
designed by architects Oscar and Oscar.

DATE SANDWICHES

Dried, chopped dates, in small, oblong, plastic packages were always in the kitchen cupboard when I was growing up. My mother baked them into cakes, I think, but I always remember them in the most curious of sandwiches. At ten years old or so, it was my wrist-breaking chore to squash them with salted butter and banana into a thick paste to spread on brown bread for "Combat Cancer" fundraising whist drives. They were held in our local Orange Hall, a small, law building red sandstone wich sat, pointedly at an elevated crossroads between three County Antrim village roads.

I was also regularly recruited for kitchen duty during the events, which I hated, despite the abundant supply of cake. Inside the hall, as the competition progressed, the air slowly thickened with cigarette smoke until, at the end of the evening, you could not see from one end of the room to the other, nor cross it without the smoke picking at the back of your throat or stabbing at your eyes. Ironic, when one considers the reason for the gathering.

The dates, I always thought, were a smart idea. Surely designed for those who, like me, could not be bothered chewing through tinned salmon, corned beef, ham and other savoury sandwiches until the apple creams and chocolate buttercream cake finally arrived with the second wave of tea.

For 4
10 minutes preparation

4 rounds of brown bread
100 g chopped dates
1 banana
75 g salted butter, softened

Mash the dates with the butter and the banana and spread on 2 slices of bread.

Put the others on top, squash them down, remove the crusts and cut into fingers. Serve with hot, black tea.

AUNTIE OLGA'S SHORTBREAD

Light, crumbly, buttery perfection.

250 g very cold salted butter, diced
330 g plain flour
85 g sugar

Pre-heat the oven to 150 °C. Put all the ingredients into the mixer (or use your fingers) and mix until you end up with a powder which looks like breadcrumbs.

Add one tablespoon of icy water and bring the mix into a ball with your hands.

Turn onto a floured surface and knead for 1 or 2 minutes until it's smooth. Press the dough into a round tin of 20cm/22cm and bake for around 45 minutes until golden on top. While the shortbread is still warm, mark out slices with a knife so it's easier to cut when completely cooled. Sprinkle with sugar before serving.

NAOMI BARS

Tagging along with my mother at Women's Institute coffee mornings and bake sales, these were the little gems I would seek out on the trays of assortments offered with our cups of strong tea and watery coffee. My mother's friend, Jean, would make them, and often a biscuit tin full of them would appear in our kitchen cupboard. They never lasted long, and in those days, the chocolate was a horrifically delicious substance called Cake Brand. Even if my 2015 version is altogether more virtuous and less industrial, apart from the dubious custard powder, perhaps, it can never compete with the taste forever imprinted in my childhood memory.

For a 23 cm tray
30 minutes preparation
1 hour resting
10 minutes cooking

For the biscuit base
150 g salted butter
150 g digestive biscuits broken into crumbs
50 g pecans or walnuts, roughly chopped
30 g desiccated coconut
1 heaped tablespoon cocoa powder

For the custard layer
125 g unsalted butter, softened
2 tablespoons custard powder
½ teaspoon vanilla extract
225 g icing sugar

For chocolate top
175 g good dark chocolate
100 g unsalted butter

Put all the ingredients of the biscuit base in a mixing bowl.

Melt the butter, pour it into the bowl and mix thoroughly.

Press the wet mixture into the tin until it is compact, but not too much or it will be difficult to cut. Put the tin in the fridge for half an hour or so to firm it up.

Beat all the ingredients for the custard base in a mixer or with a hand-held beater, until there are no lumps and it is nice and smooth. Add a little milk if it seems too solid. Spread the custard cream evenly over the biscuit base with a wide knife or a spatula and put it back into the fridge for 10 or 15 minutes.

Break the chocolate into pieces, put it in a bowl with the butter and melt over a bain-marie or gently in a microwave. Stir it carefully until the butter is well mixed through and the glaze is glossy.

Pour this over the custard layer, smooth with a spatula and leave to harden in a cool part of the kitchen, but not the fridge, which might jeopardize the shine of the chocolate.

Cut into small squares and serve with coffee or tea.

DARK TREACLE LOAF
WITH ABERNETHY BUTTER

These are everywhere you go in Ireland. The sticky blackness of the treacle and the tang of the ginger are perfect partners under a thick layer of cold salted butter. It is a loaf which is firmly a cake; there can be no toasting of it! Though it is moist enough to exist bare and alone, next to a cup of strong tea.

There are versions with wholemeal flour, some with orange juice and more than often they are studded with pieces of candied ginger. Appealing as that may be, I like the no-nonsense-ness of this one, from Kilbride Presbyterian Church's annual recipe booklet.

For 6 to 8
10 minutes preparation
1 hour 30 minutes cooking

180 g plain flour
1 level tablespoon ground ginger
½ tablespoon ground nutmeg
½ teaspoon bicarbonate of soda
2 tablespoons fresh milk
75 g treacle (2 overflowing tablespoons)
75 g golden syrup (2 overflowing tablespoons)
75 g dark muscovado
100 g salted butter
2 eggs, beaten

Pre-heat the oven to 170 °C.

Line a standard 2 lb loaf tin with a cake liner, or grease it well.

Sift the flour and spices into the bowl of the mixer. Add the sugar.

In a small cup, mix the bicarbonate of soda with the milk and set it to one side.

Warm the two syrups together in a small saucepan, stirring them so they blend together. Pour them into the flour and beat until well combined. Add the eggs, then the milk with the bicarbonate of soda, beating as you go.

Pour the mixture into the loaf tin and bake for 1 hr 15 min to 1 hr 30 min until it is well risen and firm on top.

Remove the cake from the oven and let it cool in the tin for a few minutes before turning it out onto a wire rack and cooling completely.

Leaving it in the cake lining, wrap it well in cling film and let it rest for a day or so before eating. It gets better the longer you wait.

ROCKY ROAD

A relative newcomer to the rows of traybakes and fridge cake, the rebel Yank, Rocky Road, has broken the straight-sided mould of the usual suspects and is often presented in irregular chunks. Unlike the many other sugary squares, this is one recipe where you can make a huge difference to the taste, despite the, frankly, trashy ingredients, by using really good chocolate and good quality dried fruit.

This borders on a traditional fridge cake recipe, (which is fudgier and usually covered in chocolate butter glaze) like those I recently spotted, thinly sliced, served with chocolate sauce, on a pub's dessert menu or fashioned into a Christmas Pudding shape for an "alternative" Christmas Day dessert. It might not be the most challenging or sophisticated of recipes, but it does seem as if everyone loves it.

For 10 to 12
10 minutes preparation
2 hours chilling

200 g salted butter
400 g good dark chocolate
3 tablespoons golden syrup
250 g digestive biscuits (or hobnobs or rich tea)
125 g dried raspberries, cherries, cranberries, strawberries (optional)
100 g pecans (optional)
100 g mini marshmallows

Grease and line a 20 cm x 25 cm cake tin.

Put the chocolate, butter and golden syrup in a bowl and melt gently together over a bain-marie or in the microwave.

Crush the biscuits into irregular pieces, either with a quick blast in a mini blender, or in a tea towel with a rolling pin, then add them to the chocolate mixture.

Tip in the dried fruit, marshmallows if you are using it, and stir it all well until everything is coated in chocolate.

Spread the mixture into the tin, smooth out the top and let it cool and harden in the fridge for an hour or so. Cut or break the Rocky Road into pieces and serve.

FIFTEENS

A "traybake", I am reliably informed, is a typically Northern Irish term for a large square of industrial sweetness such as those you will find on sale at filling stations, supermarkets and corner shops around the country. When I was a child, traybakes would be brought out, with tea, scones and butter, when calling on friends in rural County Antrim, and were always on sale at WI or church coffee mornings.

These days, there are some truly atrocious versions, full of rubbish confectionery and cereals, sold in garish multi packs with shelf lives as long as the lists of E numbers on their labels.

But Fifteens seem to have risen above the fray to retro cult status, joined at the counters (also in enormous portions!) of the cooler cafes by their adopted American cousin, Rocky Road. They take their name from the fifteen of each main ingredient used in the recipe. You can roll them into balls, or dip them in chocolate. I prefer them in small, round slices.

For 15 slices or so
10 minutes preparation
1 hour resting

15 glace cherries, cut in 2
15 marshmallows, cut into pieces (with scissors is easiest)
15 digestive biscuits
150 g tin condensed milk
2 tablespoons desiccated coconut

Crush the biscuits, mix in the rest of the ingredients, roll up tightly into a sausage shape in cling film and leave in the fridge for an hour or so to harden.

Slice into rounds and serve with a cup of tea or coffee.

COFFEE WALNUT BUTTERCREAM CAKE

In Ireland, you will find this cake on the menu at the best traditional tea-rooms, including a wonderful specimen at Farmgate Café in Midleton, County Cork.

These days, when I crave cake, it is this cake I crave. The combination of bitter, salty and sweet is heavenly. Thankfully, my four quarter (like the French butter sponge cake) version is quick and easy to make in an emergency.

I've used salted butter in the sponge but not in the icing here — when I was a child both would have been salted. You could do the opposite or leave it only as a little pinch with the flour.

For 8 to 10
25 minutes cooking
15 minutes preparation

250 g self raising flour
1 teaspoon baking powder
250 g salted butter, softened
250 g soft brown sugar
4 eggs
1 tablespoon very strong coffee — easiest made with instant

For icing
200 g unsalted, softened butter
500 g icing sugar
½ teaspoon vanilla extract
1 ½ tablespoons very strong coffee — easiest made with instant

30 g chopped walnuts

Pre-heat the oven to 180 °C.

Grease and line two 18 cm cake tins.

Put all the ingredients in the bowl of the mixer and beat for around one minute until the batter is smooth.

Pour the batter into the tins and smooth over the tops.

Bake for around 20 to 25 minutes, until the top of the cake is golden and puffed up. Test the centre with a knife or a skewer.

Take the tins out of the oven and leave to cool for a few minutes, then turn out and leave to cool for an hour or so.

When the cake is completely cool, beat the icing ingredients together until the icing is fluffy and well mixed.

Split the cooled cakes in two to form four discs.

Spread half the icing over three discs and set them on top of each other. Top with the final disc, ice the rest of the cake, decorate with the walnuts and leave to rest, so the icing hardens slightly, before cutting.

MAHON POINT MARKET, CORK

It is hardly the most bucolic of settings for a farmers' market: the car park and forecourt of a very large, very modern Irish suburban shopping centre. But the produce at Mahon Point Market is the very best of what Ireland's countryside can produce. The market's primary aim, set out amongst a list of very firm principles, is to support local farmers and artisans. GM foods, intensively reared meat, battery eggs, and industrially produced fruit and veg are forbidden. And the selling of organic fruit and veg and other artisanal produce from outside Ireland is restricted. There are over 40 stallholders selling an incredible array of Irish ingredients and cooked produce from shiitake mushroom powder to raw goat's milk.

There, at the crack of dawn, are Noreen and Martin Conroy, setting out their wares and finishing the cooking of the whole slow roasted hog which will be feeding the local businessmen and women popping over for a pulled pork sandwich in a few hours' time. Woodside Farm is very much a family affair, with Martin, Noreen and their five children sharing the work on their sustainably farmed land, where they rear cattle, sheep, geese, ducks and turkeys, but concentrate mainly on their herd of pedigree Gloucester Old Spot and Saddleback pigs.

The lucky pigs spend their lives outdoors, rooting about the land, their rolled wheat feed supplemented with fresh turnip, swede and kale grown on the farm. The animals are slaughtered locally and then brought back to the farm for butchering. The Conroys make and sell a fantastic range of fresh and cured pork produce, including sausages, pig's liver, kidneys, tails and caul, home-cured streaky and back bacon, as well as dry cured hams and traditional trotters, pig's cheeks and ribs.

Lemon merringues
€2 each

NEW SEASON
SPINACH
ONLY
€2

kale
only
€1·00

Cabbage
only
€1·00

kohlrabi
only
€ 1

BUNCH OF CARROTS
ONLY
€2.50

SWEDES
€1

Top right: Derek Hannon from Greenfield Farm. Bottom right: Noreen, Hannah and Martin Conroy from Woodside Farm.

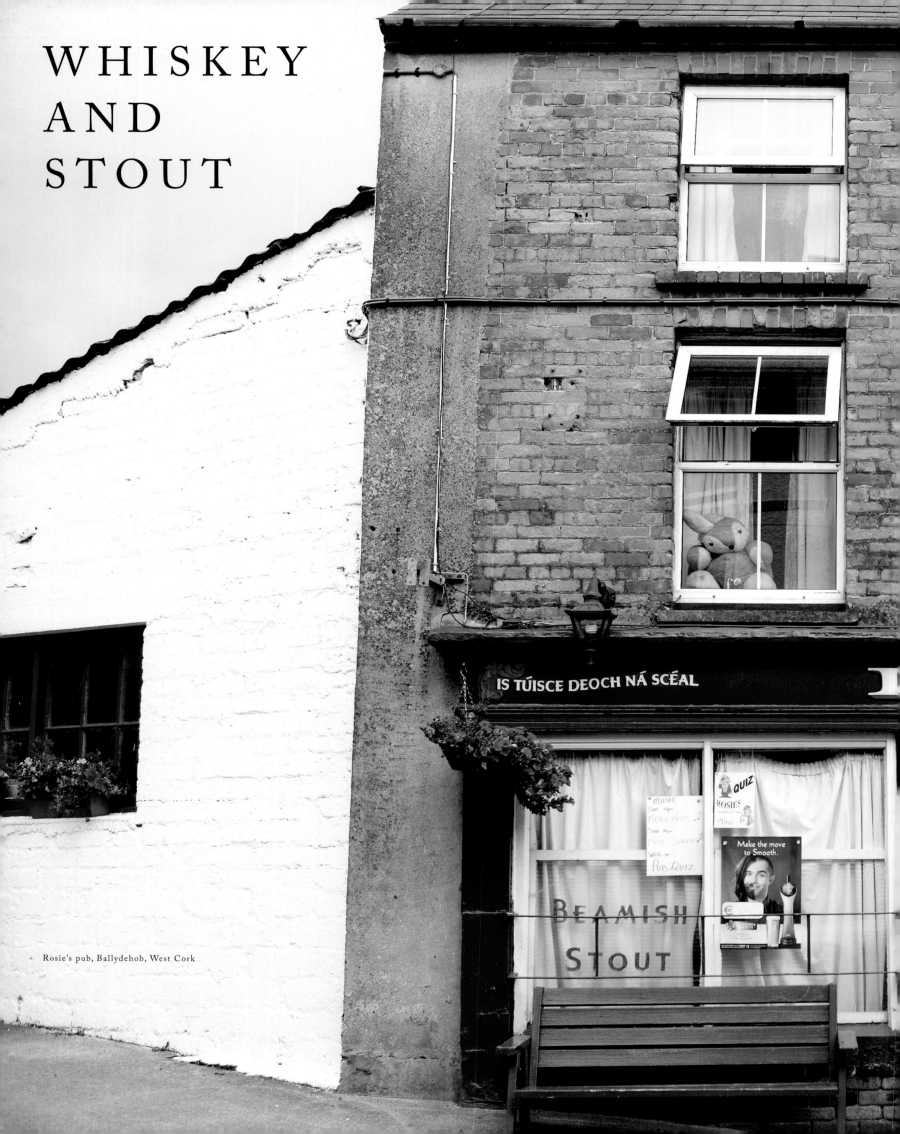

WHISKEY
AND
STOUT

Rosie's pub, Ballydehob, West Cork

IS TÚISCE DEOCH NÁ SCÉAL

BEAMISH
STOUT

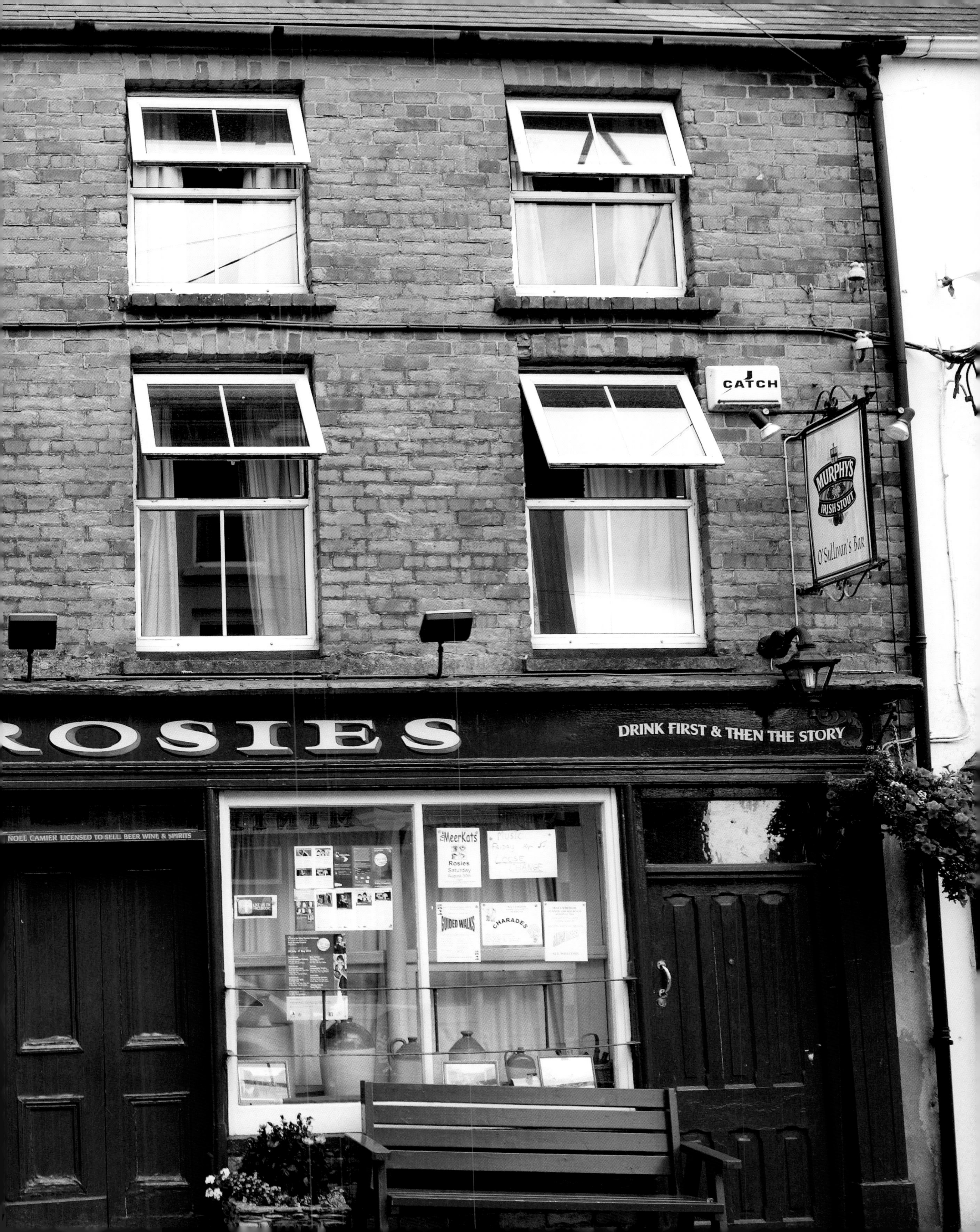

CATCH
MURPHY'S IRISH STOUT
O'Sullivan's Bar
ROSIES
DRINK FIRST & THEN THE STORY
NOEL CAMIER LICENSED TO SELL BEER WINE & SPIRITS
The MeerKats
Rosies
Saturday
Music
Friday
Loose Change
GUIDED WALKS
CHARADES

GUINNESS RAREBIT

Not the most presentable of dishes — especially with the Black Stuff colouring the cheddar a muddy brown — but it's ready in a jiffy and makes for an unbeatable high tea or late breakfast with another pint by its side.

For 4
10 minutes preparation
20 minutes cooking

50 g butter
3 tablespoons flour
200 ml Guinness
1 teaspoon English mustard
200 g mature Irish cheddar, grated
4 slices of good bread
Salt and pepper
Worcestershire sauce

Pre-heat the grill.

Melt the butter in a small, non-stick saucepan.

Add the flour and cook them together for 2 or 3 minutes, stirring with a wooden spoon, to make a roux.

Pour in the Guinness, stirring while it foams and bubbles.

Take the pan off the heat, add the mustard, then tip in the grated cheese, mixing well, to melt it through the hot sauce.

Toast the bread, spread the cheese mixture onto it, season and let it grill for a minute or so, until it browns and the cheese is bubbling.

Let it cool slightly before serving.

WHOLE BAKED ONIONS WITH BEER AND HERBS

Even softer and sweeter than the braised onions below, this is a super practical and easy way of adding meaty flavour to grilled meats.

For 6
3 minutes preparation
1 hour cooking

6 medium red onions
6 small bay leaves and/or sprigs of thyme
250 ml dark beer or Guinness
Salt and pepper

Pre-heat the oven to 180 °C. Open the tops of the onions, without peeling them, and put the herbs just inside the skin. Cut the ends off the onions so they sit flat and place them snugly in a baking dish.

Drizzle a little beer into the tops of the onions, season with salt and pepper and cover the tin tightly with foil.

Roast for 30 minutes. Take the onions out, pour in the rest of the beer, close the tin up with the foil and roast for another 20 minutes or so. Take the foil off for a final 10 minutes to allow the juices to caramelise. Season and serve hot with grilled meats whole, or with the flesh scooped out.

ONIONS IN BEER AND BUTTER

A nifty little sauce, great for steak, pork chops or as a topping for mashed potatoes, savoury oats or barley – or even as a base for an Irish *soupe a l'oignon*. The trick is to be patient enough to let them cook down and caramelise slowly. As ever, don't skimp on the butter.

For 4
5 minutes preparation
45 minutes cooking

150 g butter
750 g onions, peeled + sliced
1 tablespoon brown sugar
75 ml stout (Guinness, Murphy's)

Warm the butter in a heavy-based frying pan. Add the sliced onions and cook very slowly, stirring from time to time, until they are soft and translucent.

Add the sugar, beer and salt, and let them cook for about 45 to 50 minutes, until caramelised and almost reduced to a puree.

ONE-POT BEEF SHORT RIBS BRAISED IN GUINNESS WITH BARLEY AND ONIONS

A warming, hearty, classic Irish casserole. Serve it as it is, or with boiled potatoes or creamy champ alongside.

For 6 to 8
20 minutes preparation
4 hours cooking

2 kg beef short ribs
Salt and pepper
Vegetable oil for frying
2 onions, peeled and chopped roughly
3 carrots, peeled and chopped roughly
2 celery stalks, peeled and chopped roughly
Fresh thyme
500 ml Irish stout
Parsley, salt and pepper
50 g pearl barley

Preheat the oven to 150 °C.

Heat the oil in a large, heavy bottomed casserole dish, and brown the pieces of meat all over in a few batches, making sure not to crowd them.

Take the meat out of the pot and put it on a plate. Cook the onions, carrots, thyme, parsley and celery in the hot fat for 3 or 4 minutes, until they are softened and slightly browned.

Put the meat back in, give it all a stir, add the thyme with a little salt and pepper, then pour in the stock, scraping the bottom of the pot to pick up all the tasty bits.

Bring to the boil, cover the top of the stew with foil and pop the lid on.

Cook in the oven for 3½ hours, then remove and tip in the pearl barley.
Stir and put back into the oven (or simmer on the hob to keep an eye on proceedings). Check the seasoning and serve once the barley is soft and has given a nice creamy texture to the dish.

PUSH

inné · inniu · amárach · coicís · mí · lá
BCE ECB EZB EKT EKP 2002
scrúdú·
tnúth·
ceannach
airgead · ór
lom · dúchas

5 EURO

ENDA McEVOY

ENDA MCEVOY was born and raised in Virginia, County Cavan. After studying English and Sociology, he eventually decided to make cooking his career. McEvoy travelled to Spain, Germany and the UK to train, before returning to Galway. He worked at Nimmo's Restaurant and then at cheesemonger and passionate local food activist Seamus Sheridan's restaurant, Sheridan's on the Docks. Seamus gave Enda all the free rein and financial assistance he could want, recognising his talent and passion for Irish *terroir*, in particular the foraging of its wild plants. When Sheridan's was sadly forced to close, Enda went to Copenhagen to train with Rene Redzepi in the world's best restaurant, Noma. While working there, he was approached to come work in Galway's groundbreaking restaurant, Aniar. In 2012, Aniar was awarded a Michelin star, hugely boosted by McEvoy's interpretation of new, modern Irish cooking and Nordic cuisine. It was a massive achievement for such a young and daring enterprise. To everyone's surprise, Enda left soon after, and his own baby, again associated with Seamus Sheridan, is the sparsely beautiful and unique Loam. Conor Cockram, Enda's sous-chef, has similarly impressive credentials, having worked at Sketch Pierre Gagnaire for two years, and cut his teeth at Pierre Gagnaire, rue de Balzac, Paris, The Ledbury, Le Manoir aux Quat'Saisons, Hibiscus, The Greenhouse and Dinner by Heston Blumenthal. Conor met Enda while he was working in Sheridan's on the Docks and went on with him to Aniar in late 2011. Passionate about foraging wild plants and finding new ways of using indigenous Irish produce, he is now bringing all his talents to Loam, alongside Enda.

GUINNESS AND OYSTERS, A MATCH MADE IN IRELAND

In the 19th century, oysters were popular and inexpensive. Served for less than the price of peanuts today, their saltiness kept people drinking. The dark creaminess and roasted bitter taste of stout goes so well with the oysters' brininess, and its mild carbonation lifts the flavours off the tongue.

The two are such a perfect match (though it is rumoured, outside Ireland, that champagne, sake and a good Muscadet come very close) that stout makers have experimented with adding oyster flesh into the brewing process. Many see this as just a gimmick, adding barely a note of brine and ultimately taking away from the taste of both oyster and stout. GQ beer writer Willian Bostwick quipped, "You wouldn't make a Coke that tastes like a Big Mac, would you?"

SUPER SIMPLE RAW RHUBARB CONDIMENT

Great with raw oysters, salmon and mackerel.

For 4
10 minutes preparation
5 minutes cooking

2 stalks rhubarb
1 tablespoon sugar
Lemon juice (optional)

Cut the rhubarb into 2 cm chunks (saving 2 to chop raw), put it in a saucepan and sprinkle with sugar.

Add a tablespoon or two of water and heat, lid on.

Let it cook as it produces its own steam, checking the heat so it doesn't burn or dry out.

Cook for 3 or 4 minutes, until the fruit is soft. Strain the juice (keep the pulp for pudding!) and let it cool.

Dice the raw rhubarb very finely and mix with the juice.

Check the taste and add a squeeze of lemon if it needs sprucing up.
Spoon a little into each oyster shell.

SEAWEED RELISH
FOR OYSTERS

A great little condiment for spicing up oysters. Serve with brown or rye bread and salted butter.

For 6
10 minutes preparation

250 g fresh or rehydrated mixed seaweed
6 small shallots
2 tablespoons cider vinegar
2 tablespoons rapeseed oil

Chop the seaweed finely and mix it with the other ingredients.

Leave to rest before serving with the oysters.

SEAWEED BUTTER
OYSTER TOASTIE

Thanks to French chef Guy Savoy for this brilliant idea, from his tiny oyster bar in Paris, L'Huitrade, which showcases the best oyster producers from France's shores. We need one of these in every Irish town, please.

For 4
15 minutes preparation
3 to 4 minutes cooking

4 slices good white pan bread.
150 g salted butter (yup)
1 heaped tablespoon dried seaweed flakes or fresh, diced seaweed.
Zest of a lemon, pepper to taste
About 8 meaty oysters, freshly shucked + drained

Chop the oysters into small pieces, drain again or set onto kitchen paper if they are too wet.

Whizz 100 g of the butter in a mini processor with the seaweed. Season with the lemon zest and pepper.

Spread the seaweed butter on one side of each slice of bread, keeping a little over for the hot, finished product, and spread the plain butter on the other side, but more lightly. Set the bread seaweed butter side up and spoon the chopped oyster onto two halves, leaving a little space around the sides.

Close the sandwiches firmly with the other two slices of buttered bread, then toast in a sandwich maker until golden and bubbling. If you don't have one of these magic contraptions (a must in any house with ravenous teens like mine) try to seal the sandwiches the best you can and fry them gently in the pan.

Serve immediately with the rest of the butter. They are simply mind-blowing with a pint of Guinness.

GUINNESS CHOCOLATE CARAMEL WAFFLES

A little nip of Guinness in this sauce balances the sweetness nicely, and as always with Guinness, dances well with a good, dark chocolate. If you get the waffles right — crisp outside, spongy inside — it's a dessert bordering on sophisticated. As ever, I like some loosely whipped, cooling double cream to calm all the chocolaty excitement, but good vanilla or milk ice cream would also do the job very well indeed.

For 8 waffles or so
5 minutes preparation
40 minutes cooking

For the waffles
200 g plain flour
50 g cocoa powder
1 tablespoon baking powder
50 g sugar
3 eggs, yolks separated from the whites
300 ml milk
125 ml vegetable oil

For the sauce
100 g sugar
50 g salted butter
Splash of Guinness (about 100 ml)
2 tablespoons thick double cream
200 g good dark chocolate

Start by making the sauce. Heat the sugar in a heavy bottomed saucepan until it starts to caramelise. Turn the saucepan so that the hot sugar (be careful!) caramelises equally without burning.

Add the butter and the Guinness and stir constantly. The pan will spit and splutter. Again, take care not to burn yourself. Add the cream, still stirring until you have a smooth sauce. Remove from the heat and add the chocolate, stirring until it is melted.

If the sauce is too thick, add a little more cream until you have the consistency you like. Leave it to cool as you make the waffles.

Sift the flour, cocoa powder and baking sugar into a bowl.

Beat the milk and the egg yolks together with the oil.

Make a well in the centre of the flour and pour in the liquid, whisking as you go until the batter is smooth.

Whisk the egg whites until they form soft peaks, then fold them into the chocolate batter.

Heat the waffle iron and cook the waffles for about 3 minutes until they are set. The cooking time does depend on your machine, even more so than pancakes, so the first attempt may not be presentable! But once the iron is at the correct temperature you will get into your stride.

GOOD THINGS CAFE PORTER CAKE

Chef owner Carmel Somers writes : "This is the most asked for recipe at the cafe and cookery class. We always have one on the go for the students to pick at during the week. One student emailed me last week to say she made it in the morning, had some friends around in the evening and the cake was eaten. I was given this recipe by Mary Keane of Keanes bar (the nicest bar in Ireland) in the Maam valley in County Galway years ago, and I have made many of them since, as well as a couple for weddings. It is so easy, you cannot go wrong. The cake to make for the non baker."

For 12
60 minutes preparation
120 minutes cooking

500 g plain flour
1 teaspoon mixed spice
225 g butter
225g soft brown sugar
1 level teaspoon of bread soda
4 eggs lightly beaten
450 g currants
450 g sultanas
1 bottle of stout (dark beer)

In a large saucepan, mix together the mixed spice, butter and sugar and add ½ of the stout.

Heat the mixture gently and let it simmer lightly until everything has melted. Next add the fruit.

Mix the rest of the stout with the bread soda and combine with the beaten eggs, then add to the mixture in the saucepan and finally fold in the flour.

Bake in a lined 25 cm round tin at 150 °C for about 2 hours, until tested in the centre with a knife and it comes out clean

Do check from time to time in case the top is burning. If so, turn the oven down to suit.

IRISH COFFEE

A steady hand and good cream are necessary for one of our best known national drinks.
So many imposters and interpretations exist, it feels good to bring it back to basics here.
The most important thing to strive for in a good Irish coffee is the balance of temperature and texture.
The hot, sweet whiskey coffee base must not have a trace of sugar crunch, and the cold cream atop
it must be thick yet still pourably liquid. Only then can you fully appreciate the joy of sipping hot,
boozy coffee through a moustache of cold cream.

I commit the terrible crime of liking the coffee in my Irish coffee to be very strong indeed, hence
the espresso in the photo even if it does mean the foam from the coffee can interfere
with an immaculate creamy layer. Good filter coffee is really what you're after here.

For 2
5 minutes preparation

2 measures of whiskey (70 ml)
2 heaped teaspoons Demerara sugar
400 ml good coffee
4 to 5 tablespoons whipping cream

Whisk the cream slightly so that it is thick and slightly aerated but will still pour, not until it is stiff
and immobile.

Warm two Irish coffee glasses — usually they have a stem and a handle — with boiling water.

Put the sugar into the glasses and add a little hot coffee. Stir well until the sugar is completely dissolved.
Pour the coffee to fill the glasses to about 2/3.

Set a teaspoon, most have it filling side up, some down, onto the surface of the coffee, so that the tip is
touching the inside edge of the glass. Pour the cream onto the spoon, allowing it to flow widely and slowly
onto the surface of the coffee, without sinking into it. Fill the glass to the brim and serve immediately.

Do not stir! Never stir.

WHISKEY TRIFLE WITH COUNTRY CHOICE VANILLA POACHED PLUMS

Every Irish household has their own version of this pudding, flavoured with the devil brew and tinged with sin, and there are many nudge-nudge, wink-wink stories of old aunties and the disappearing cooking sherry, or teetotal Sister Bernadettes tucking into third helpings when the family trifle appeared at Sunday lunch.

My own memories of childhood trifles are typically Presbyterian — a thin layer of cream over packet custard, both atop raspberry jelly, with the odd slice of banana or cube of tinned peach suspended in it, set hard over a layer of sodden, tasteless trifle sponge. If there was sherry, well, it must have been reserved for the grown-ups' version and certainly never passed my lips. But then it has to be said that trifle was unfashionable in the convenience-crazy, "continental cuisine" days of the 1970s and 1980s, and in our house it was all *crêpe suzette* and *crème caramel*. It is only in its glorious revived incarnations of the past decade or so that trifle's appeal has been adequately appreciated. For when the ingredients are good, and the cook's hand is generous and uninhibited, the combination of whiskey-soaked sponge, tart fruit, eggy custard and proper fresh cream is a fabulous one. (Delahunt restaurant in Dublin makes the best I have ever tasted.)

Undoubtedly traumatised by the austere trifles of my youth, I have always preferred to skip the jelly altogether and rely on poached fruit alone. In Country Choice's jars of vanilla poached plums, the syrup is usually abundant and intense, not too sweet, and handy for thoroughly soaking the sponge, alongside the whiskey. In my house, homemade custard is an absolute must, as is a top-heavy layer of cream and retro glace or maraschino cherries for decoration. I've also given you an "Irish Cranachan" version with raspberry, whiskey and oats.

For 8 to 10
45 minutes preparation
30 minutes cooking

For the custard
450 ml double cream
5 egg yolks
50 g sugar
1 tablespoon cornflour
1 vanilla pod
5 trifle sponges (or a dozen or so ladyfingers)
3 tablespoons plum, cherry or raspberry jam
150 ml good Irish whiskey
500 g poached red plums (or cherries or raspberries or a mixture of these)

300 ml double cream
1 heaped tablespoon mascarpone (optional)

Start by making the custard, as it will take time to cool and set. Bring the cream to the boil with the vanilla pod split in half lengthways. Meanwhile, whisk the egg yolks with the sugar and cornflour until they turn pale and double in volume.

Pour the hot cream into the eggs, whisk until it is mixed and smooth, then pour it all back into the saucepan and heat again, stirring constantly.

When the custard starts to thicken, lower the heat whilst continuing to stir. Once it is of setting consistency, take the pan off the heat, set some cling film on the surface of the custard to avoid a skin forming, and leave it to cool completely.

Cut the trifle sponges in two and spread them with the jam. Set them into the bottom of a pretty glass bowl. Put the plums with their syrup into a bowl, add the whiskey and stir through. Pour the boozy fruit onto the trifle sponges and leave to rest.

Once the custard has cooled, spread it over the fruit and sponge. Whisk the cream with the mascarpone, if you are using it, and leave to rest in the fridge for at least 2 or 3 hours.

Decorate with glace or maraschino cherries.

RASPBERRY AND HONEY TRIFLE WITH TOASTED OATS AND WHISKEY

Make up the custard as for the plum trifle.

Toast a handful of porridge oats with some sugar in the oven and let them cook completely.

Crush 250 g of raspberries with a little icing sugar so as their juice runs (you can also heat them for a minute or two and let them cool) and spread them over the trifle sponges. Sprinkle the whiskey over the fruit and let it all soak in nicely. Tumble a further 250 g/300 g of fresh raspberries (keep a few over for decoration) on the crushed layer, and cover with the cooled custard.

Whisk the cream and mascarpone with 2 tablespoons of runny Irish honey and top the custard with it.

Decorate with the toasted oats and a few more raspberries and serve.

BAILEYS CHOCOLATE CAKE WITH COFFEE CHOCOLATE GANACHE

Baileys Irish Cream was one of the first alcoholic drinks I tasted. I remember sipping it surreptitiously from my parents' drinks cabinet as a teen and wondering why on earth we were supposed to be grown-up to enjoy booze. It was so sweet it felt entirely harmless.

These days, I like to drink it on ice, and can usually only manage one, as my adult tastebuds seem slowly to be turning off sugar these days. In desserts and baking, however, it's a good pal, here adding even more moistness to an already dense chocolate cake. If I were you, I'd try the (outrageously rich) chocolate version in a Tiramisu.

For 8 to 10
10 minutes preparation
40 minutes cooking

150 g salted butter
100 g good dark chocolate
200 g sugar
2 tablespoons good quality cocoa powder
150 ml Baileys liqueur
175 g plain flour
2 teaspoons baking powder
3 eggs lightly beaten

For the chocolate ganache
200 g dark chocolate
100 g unsalted butter
1 tablespoon very strong coffee (made with instant granules is easiest)

Pre-heat the oven to 170 °C.

Grease and line a 20/21 cm cake tin.

Melt the chocolate, butter, sugar, cocoa powder and Baileys together over a bain-marie or in the microwave. Stir until smooth and leave to cool.

Add the eggs to the mixture and then sift in the flour and baking powder.

Fold to combine, and pour the batter into the prepared tin.

Bake for around 40 minutes, until the sides no longer wobble when you shake the tin, but the middle still appears slightly soft and molten.

Take the cake out of the oven and let it cool for 5 minutes or so, then turn it out onto a wire rack.

When it is completely cool, make the ganache. Put the chocolate, butter and water into a bowl and melt gently over a bain-marie or in the microwave. Stir lightly until the glaze is glossy.

Let it cool and thicken for a few minutes before glazing the cake.

Leave to set.

Serve as dessert with double cream and good coffee.

THE MIDLETON BRICK,
BY KEVIN AHERNE, SAGE

This dessert is a derivative from the French verb *pavé*, meaning a brick or cobblestone used to make a firm, level surface. This year, we have been fortunate enough in my home town of Midleton to have a new organic chocolatier along with a great supplier of eggs for the marshmallow topping.

Hence the name The Midleton Brick!

This recipe is broken down into 3 parts then assembled. Follow the stages in order

For 6
2 hours preparation
30 minutes cooking

For the feuillantine pastry
110 g butter
110 g icing sugar
110 g egg whites
110 g plain flour or gluten free flour

For the chocolate brick
300 g dark chocolate (70% cacao)
3 eggs + 3 egg (whites go in the marshmallows)
120 g honey
 300 g semi-whipped cream

For the marshmallow
190 g caster sugar
1 teaspoon glucose powder
125 g water
3 leaves gelatine
1 teaspoon vanilla extract
3 eggs whites

Make the feuillantine pastry: cream the butter and the sugar, slowly add the egg whites, then fold in the flour. Spread on a baking sheet and bake at 180 °C until golden brown (6-8 minutes). Leave to cool, then crumble the mixture so as to use like the base of a cheesecake. Spread evenly across a greased bread tin (a cheesecake tin will do). You won't get the brick shape with the cheesecake tin but it will taste just as good.

Make the chocolate brick: melt the chocolate in a bowl over steaming water. In a separate pot, bring the honey up to the boil. Slowly add the honey to the melted chocolate in a separate bowl. Whisk the eggs in the same bowl until light and fluffy. Add the chocolate mixture slowly then fold in the semi-whipped cream. Pour the mixture into your bread or cheesecake tin on top of the pastry.

Make the marshmallow: add the gelatine to the water for 5 minutes, then remove. Bring the glucose and water to the boil. Add the gelatine, and whisk until dissolved In a mixer, whisk the egg whites until they start turning white. Very slowly add the syrup mixture. You will see the mixture start to fluff up like meringue. When you have finished pouring in the mixture, add the vanilla essence. Pour the mixture on top of your chocolate brick and leave to set for at least 6 hours. The marshmallow works very well toasted in this dish, so if you have access to a blow torch, give it a quick toast on top. Otherwise, a quick flash under a hot grill will do. It makes all the difference. Carefully remove from the tin, cut into 6 slices and serve.

CUCUMBER, ELDERFLOWER AND GIN COCKTAIL

The artisan gin revival of recent years has not spared Ireland, thankfully. Our *terroir* produces such pure water and wonderful cocktails of botanicals, that would surely be a sin to leave all the gin to the English. The highly aromatic Shortcross Gin from Northern Ireland, and the brand new, crisp London Dry Blackwater Gin from Waterford are the stars of the moment, contributing to a heightened interest and change in tastes.

This simple cocktail bumps up the floral and grassy notes of gin with sweet elderflower and refreshes the palate with icy cucumber.

For 2
2 to 3 hours freezing for the cucumber
5 minutes preparation

40 ml gin
Dash of elderflower cordial
2/3 cucumber, peeled
100 ml still lemonade
Tonic or soda water
Lemon zest
Lemon and cucumber slices for garnish

Peel the cucumber and puree it in a mini blender. Freeze the pulp in ice cubes or in a small food container.

When the cucumber is frozen, put a couple of cubes per person with the gin, elderflower cordial, still lemon and zest into a cocktail shaker and shake vigourously for 15 seconds or so.

Pour into glasses, top up with tonic or soda to your taste and garnish with slices of lemon and cucumber.

IRISH WHISKEY

Pernod Ricard® completely revolutionized the way young people drink whiskey around the world when they bought Ireland's only two distilleries Bushmills and Midleton in the 80s and made Jameson into a spirit just like rum or vodka, to be enjoyed as a base alcohol in mixed drinks and cocktails.

Since those days there has been a revival in traditional pure pot still whiskey, drunk on its own — neat, with ice or cold water — and enjoyed for its flavour. Until 2014 there were still only four distilleries, now there are over fifteen, with new craft distilleries springing up all the time.

My favourite Irish whiskey remains Black Bush, a blend from Bushmills, with a high triple distilled malt content, aged in Oloroso sherry casks for eight to ten years. When I read how it is described by drinks writer David Wondrich, I understand more why I love it so much. "A classic blend, heavy on the malt. Like liquid angel-food cake, smooth and grainy."

Whiskey that tastes like cake? Of course!

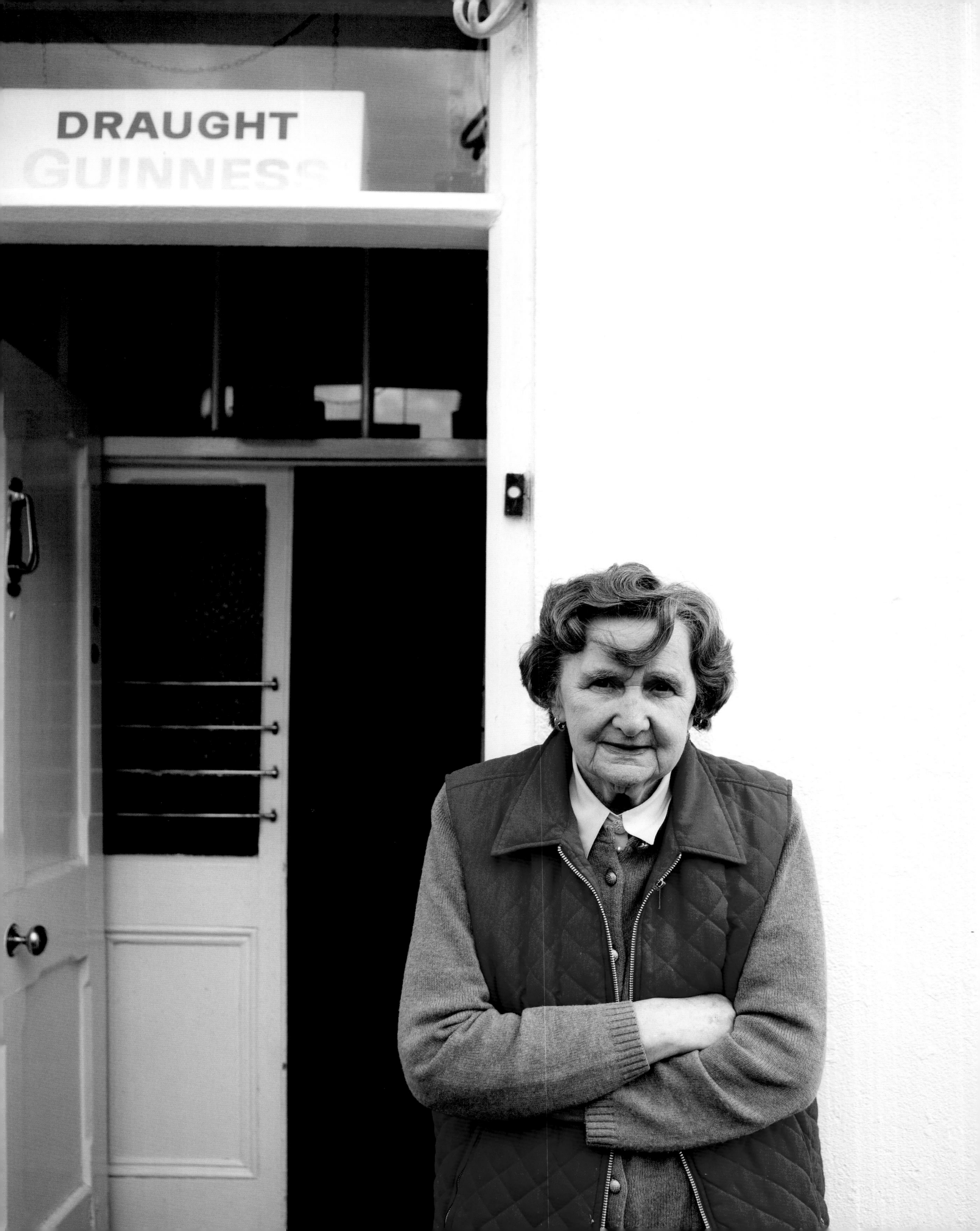
DRAUGHT
GUINNESS

PUBS

In parts of rural Ireland, the traditional village pub is the social and community hub, although many are closing down fast. This is where local people come to indulge in Ireland's favourite pastime, talking, catching up on the day's news from each other, not from an ever-switched-on TV screen perched in the corner. Drink is taken as a kind of punctuation to the tales being told. Some liken it to a confession box, or a therapist's couch. This is where villagers gather after funerals, christenings and weddings, and where the man or woman behind the bar (most likely the son or daughter of the previous bartender) needs to know all about you before your lips make contact with your pint of Guinness. "You go into a pub abroad and they'd just, they'd nearly ignore you," says Paul Gartlan, Kingscourt, Co. Cavan, appearing in the charming 2014 documentary *The Irish Pub* by Alex Fegan. "You go into a pub in Ireland and they'd go up in your arse to find out who you are." As social trends change, and drinking and smoking laws tighten, many of these old style family pubs are being lost forever. Sometimes known as "spirit groceries" (up to the 1960s), bars fulfilled many functions, from general store to cobbler, to mortuary. The large counter space with roomy shelves, with snugs for those wanting to sit and stay a while was their typical layout inside. Very often, a village pub is an extension of the owner's home and there is little distinction between the bar and the lived-in warmth of their front room. But unlike modern bars, and many pseudo Irish style pubs so loved around the world, there is no music, no TV and no food served.

Still, to survive, many of Ireland's pubs must adapt. And today, laying on Irish food and music is what seems to be required to stay afloat. Thankfully there are hundreds of places around the country where your night out includes a good meal, and some great craic, even if no-one knows you or will remember your name the next day.

Ina Daly in front of her pub, Daly's, Ballydehob, West Cork.

Top right, bottom right and left: Daly's pub, Ballydehob. Top left: pub in Donnybrook, Dublin.

100 IRISH ADDRESSES

Like the recipes that precede it, this is an imperfect, incomplete and idiosyncratic list. But these are quite simply my favourite places in Ireland — so far, there are so many more I want to discover ! — and I wanted to share them with you.

The North, Sligo & Donegal

Bushmills Inn, Bushmills

A Causeway Coast institution, the original heart of this ancient coaching inn is still intact, and if you can nab the seats in front of the open hearth you might stay all evening with a few Guinnesses.

bushmillsinn.com

9 Dunluce Road, Bushmills, County Antrim BT57 8QG

The French Rooms, Bushmills

Wind your way through a lot of French-themed giftware (or stop to shop if that's your thing) and get down the back to where the good coffee, tea, toast and scones are.

thefrenchrooms.com

45 Main Street, Bushmills BT57 8QA

Babushka, Portrush

An old ice cream parlour has been converted into a super cool cafe. Here there's good coffee (infuriatingly hard to find along the North Coast), bread from Ursa Minor bakery in Ballycastle and fresh food made on the premises.

facebook.com/babushkafoods

South Pier, Portrush BT56

Lost and Found, Coleraine

Coleraine discovers hip! Groovy vibe, terrific coffee, lovely décor.

wearelostandfound.com

2 Queen Street, Coleraine BT52 1BE

Harry's Shack, Portstewart

A shining beacon of pitch-perfect flavour, great service and terrific value in Northern Ireland's most touristic region. The laid back shack is cosy when it's chilly, yet open and airy enough to let the outside in when the sun shines.

facebook.com/HarrysShack

116 Strand Road, Portstewart BT55 7PG

Balloo House, Killinchy

Chef Danny Millar's 400 year old coaching house has a laid-back bistro on the ground floor and a more formal upstairs dining room. Along with his new gastropub, the Poachers Pocket in nearby Lisbane, and the already thriving Parson's Nose, he is rapidly becoming the king of upmarket pub grub in the north.

ballooinns.com

Balloo House, 1 Comber Road Killinchy Newtownards

Bennetts, Belfast

High ceilings and diner — like booths make this cafe a pleasant place to dawdle over coffee or one of their excellent milk shakes. But its fantastic Belfast Fish pie, all creamy and smoky and crispily-topped with a good, punchy Irish cheddar, is what will bring me back again.

+44 28 9065 6590

4 Belmont Road, Belfast, County Antrim

Home Restaurant, Belfast

Here the veg is mostly organic, grown locally and treated with the respect it deserves by Home's young chefs. Part of the Mourne Seafood mini-group, Home understands today's Belfast crowd perfectly. Fantastic value, great service, packed out, urban and buzzy — everything Belfast does extremely well.

homebelfast.co.uk

22 Wellington Place, Belfast BT1 6GE

OX, Belfast

OX's opening heralded a new era of dining in Belfast. With its sister ship, the OX Cave wine bar next door, two airy, relaxed spaces run into each other, allowing a long evening of great wines, guided by Alain Kerloc'h and masterfully creative cooking from chef Stevie Toman. The tasting menu is a revelation of local Northern Irish produce, and a superb display of Stevie's talent.

oxbelfast.com

1 Oxford Street, Belfast BT1 3LA

The Merchant Bar, Belfast

Deep red velvet banquettes and low armchairs, antique Baccarat chandeliers and no standing at the bar make this the sexiest, most grown-up spot for serious cocktails in town.

themerchanthotel.com

16 Skipper Street, Belfast, County Antrim BT1 2DZ,

Muriel's Cafe Bar, Belfast

Housed in a former brothel, with rows of lingerie as indoor bunting, Muriel's is the funkiest bar in town with expert barmen and a grand list of finest gins.

facebook.com/muriels.cafebar

12-14 Church Lane, Belfast BT1 4QN

The Spaniard Bar, Belfast

Another great little bar, dark and full of quirky knick-knacks, just beside the Merchant hotel, here the speciality is rum. The knowledgeable staff can guide you through over 60 varieties.

thespaniardbar.com

3 Skipper Street, Belfast, County Antrim BT1 2DZ

The Crown Bar, Belfast

A gem of Victorian décor and architecture, with its orate ceramics, gas lighting and cosy snugs, The Crown is now owned by The National Trust. Do try the ales but the pub grub is sadly very ordinary.

nationaltrust.org.uk/crown-bar/

46 Great Victoria Street, Belfast, County Antrim BT2 7BA

Mourne Seafood Bar, Belfast

A terrific fish and seafood restaurant and shop in the newly renovated pedestrian Bank Square. A Belfast classic, not to be missed when you're after oysters and good fresh fish.

mourneseafood.com

34-36 Bank Street, Belfast BT1 1HL

St Georges Market, Belfast

A jewel in Belfast's food crown, this beautiful old sandstone building, with its high, skylit roof, has housed a thriving market since the 1890s. Now the fresh fish, vegetable and meat stalls are joined by a huge choice of sit in or takeaway food vendors, from filled Belfast baps to veggie curries. Go to the Variety Market early on Friday mornings with the chefs and locals in the know.

Friday Variety Market: 6 am - 2 pm

Saturday: City Food and Craft Market 9 am - 3 pm

Sunday: Market (a mix of Friday and Saturday) 10 am - 4 pm

12-20 East Bridge Street, Belfast, Antrim BT1 3NQ

Nancy's Bar, Ardara, Donegal

Probably my favourite bar in Ireland. Lots of nooks and crannies, unspoiled décor and open fires, good oysters, terrific Guinness and incomparable music and craic. There's always something happening, or someone new in town to chat to. Nancy's is welcoming, warm and lively all year long, even in the heart of a harsh Donegal winter.

nancysardara.com

Front Street, Ardara, Co. Donegal

Harry's Bridgend, Donegal

Superb chef and Donegal man Derek Creagh is now in residence at Harry's in Bridgend, and the starry reviews are flooding in! Using the best of the superb local produce from their walled garden, Greencastle fishing boats and Inishowen peninsula, Creagh's cooking is not to be missed.

facebook.com/pages/Harrys-Restaurant

Harrys, Bridgend, Donegal

Shells Cafe, Strandhill, Sligo

A surfing lifestyle heaven, this sunny, fun cafe and shop right by the majestic Strandhill beach sells the best fish and chips in the region. Coffee, cakes and cafe food are all super too. The perfect place to warm up and chill out after a bracing day at the beach.

shellscafe.com

Seafront, Strandhill, Co. Sligo

The Counter Deli, Letterkenny

The super cheerful and clued-in owner Richard Finney will happily guide you through his good list of craft beers ans wines. There's also excellent coffee, cheese, breas, cured meats ans smoked fish to take away.

thecounterdeli.com

Canal Road, Letterkenny.

The Old Schoolhouse Inn, Comber

Will Brown's sharp, modern cooking has been winning hil accolades in this peaceful, tucked away corner of Co. Down. Unbeatable value for the best of Northern Irish produce, with lovely service. Go.

100 Ballydrain Road,

Castle Espie, Co. Down

theoldschoolhouseinn.com

Dublin and surrounding area

Restaurant Forty One, Dublin

Graham Neville rules Dublin dining right now. Every new menu oozes his growing poise and handling of some great local produce. Restaurant 41's plush rooms and comfy chairs are good for lingering lunches and romantic evenings.

restaurantfortyone.ie

Residence, 41 St Stephen's Green, Dublin 2

Brother Hubbard, Dublin

Vibrant soups, sandwiches and salads, gorgeous cakes and terrific coffee. This pocket sized, owner run, independent cafe is one of the best in town.

brotherhubbard.ie

153 Capel Street, Dublin 1

Delahunt, Dublin

A new kid in town in 2015, Delahunt's beautiful rooms and plucky Irish cuisine immediately made it Dublin's hottest reservation. There are seats along the very swish bar, and roomier tables at the back, but the window booth is worth waiting for.

delahunt.ie

39, Camden Street Lower, Dublin 2

Etto, Dublin

Such a sunny place to eat, even on the rainiest Dublin night. The accomplished Med-feeling mix of tapas-style nibbles, good wines and lovely puddings, along with lovely service, gives Etto such an energetic buzz.

etto.ie

18 Merrion Row, Dublin 2

The Greenhouse, Dublin

Serious fine dining from Mickael Viljanen, in a luxurious if rather austere room, that I much prefer at night than at lunchtime. If you go for the impressive tasting menu, cancel lunch that day and breakfast the next.

Dawson St, Dublin 2 Dawson St, Dublin 2

thegreenhouserestaurant.ie

Forest Avenue, Dublin

A husband and wife team cooking in what they call a "neighbourhood dining room" and turning out some of the most creative cooking in Dublin at the moment.

forestavenuerestaurant.ie

8-9 Sussex Terrace, Dublin 4

The Mulberry Garden, Dublin

Tucked away off the street in residential (and foodie) Donnybrook, the Mulberry Garden promises contemporary Irish fine dining, and delivers it well. Quite a formal room, decorated with Irish fabrics and paintings from Irish artists.

mulberrygarden.ie

Mulberry Lane, Donnybrook, Dublin

The Woollen Mills Eating House, Dublin

In a fabulous location, just at the foot of Dublin's charming Ha'penny Bridge, the Woollen Mills has arguably the coolest outdoor seating for watching the world go by in Dublin. Inside, it's all communal tables, exposed wires and pipes and modern Irish bistro food, with a takeout patisserie and coffee shop at one end.

thewoollenmills.com

42 Lower Ormond Quay, Dublin 1

The Pig's Ear, Dublin

A consistently good value and inventive Irish menu on offer here, with rather beautiful — if, in the evening, very large! — plates of food showcasing some of the country's best produce. Bang in the centre, a stone's throw from Trinity and St Stephen's Green.

thepigsear.com
4 Nassau St, Dublin, Co. Dublin City

Sophie's, The Dean Hotel, Dublin

Even if the food has yet to live up to it, this properly breathtaking room — a pretty successful mash-up of Soho House and Ace Hotel in NYC, perched high over Dublin's rooftops, with large windows on all sides "where the weather is the wallpaper" — is an absolute must as the sun goes up (for breakfast) or down (for cocktails).

deanhoteldublin.ie
33 Harcourt Street, Dublin 2

Dunne and Crescenzi, Dublin

Eileen Dunne-Crescenzi's Italian restaurant started life as a wine shop, and although you can still browse the shelves filled with Italian wines, this is the place to come in Dublin for good, authentic Italian food and coffee.

dunneandcrescenzi.com
16 Frederick Street South, Dublin

Alchemy Juice Company, Dublin

Perched above Grafton Street in Brown Thomas' smaller department store, with floor to ceiling windows, this is the perfect spot for people-watching in Dublin. It's also where to come for an ultra-clean, vitamin top-up of juices, salads and everything a modern food health worshipper (or just a hangover nurser) might crave.

alchemyjuice.ie
2nd Floor, 28a Grafton St, Dublin

Hatch and Sons, Dublin

In a cute, light basement room on the edge of St Stephen's Green, Hatch and Sons serves only traditional, top quality Irish produce. It's not cheap, but a good place to come for the best Irish breakfast and decent coffee.

hatchandsons.co
15 St Stephen's Green, Dublin

The Cliff Townhouse, Dublin

My favourite place to go for breakfast in Dublin. Crisp linens, silver teapots and deep banquettes enhance a terrific choice of carefully executed Irish specialities. The porridge is good, the fruit freshly cut, the smoked salmon tip top, and they will make your eggs and coffee exactly the way you require. No mean feat these days.

22 St Stephen's Green, Dublin 2
theclifftownhouse.com

Fallon and Byrne, Dublin

Over three floors of a bold and beautiful sandstone building, Fallon and Byrne serves up the best of Dublin. On the ground floor is a Dean and DeLuca-esque food hall, with coffee shop , excellent butchers and cheese counter. Below is the vast wine bar, where you can order a glass or two to go with their menu, or something taken away from the deli upstairs. On the third floor is a huge restaurant, serving the modern European usuals with an Irish twist or two.

fallonandbyrne.com
11-17 Exchequer St, Dublin 2

Tankardstown House, Co. Meath

Head chef Robbie Krawczyk's sensational cooking has caused quite a stir and brought Dubliners well out of their usual gastro stomping grounds to this luxurious country house. Robbie's fine-dining tasting menu is served in the (still quite informal feeling) Brabazon restaurant, or there's a more pub grubbish offering in the Cellar.

tankardstown.ie
Tankardstown, Co. Meath

Sheridans, Kells, Co. Meath

Founded in 1995, when brothers Seamus and Kevin Sheridan started selling cheese at Galway market, there are now four stores across Ireland and six market stalls. The largest is housed in Kells, in an old railway station building, with a cafe and food shop. Sheridans cheese shop in Dublin is bang in the heart of the shopping centre, on South Anne Street.

sheridanscheesemongers.com
Virginia Road Station, Pottlereagh, Kells, Co. Meath
11 South Anne Street, Dublin 2

Brown Hound Bakery, Drogheda

Situated in an extremely unlikely spot — in the middle of a housing estate on the outskirts of Drogheda — this bakery is nonetheless worth making a detour for. The gorgeous cakes, scones and biscuits are excellent, and beautifully displayed on vintage cake stands amongst cute bric-a-brac and Irish craft, some of it for sale

facebook.com/pages/Brown-Hound-Bakery-Ireland
Bryanstown Centre, Dublin Rd, Drogheda, Co. Louth

Fumbally, Dublin

The grooviest cafe in Dublin, housed in a lovely, airy space with big, roomy tables. Really good, simple food, mostly organic fruit and veg and excellent cakes, juices and coffee.

thefumbally.ie
Fumbally Lane, Dublin 8

The South: Kilkenny to Bantry

Idaho Cafe, Cork City

Super friendly, funky cafe serving terrific coffee, lovely fish pie and cake, bang in the centre of Cork, near the town's poshest shop, Brown Thomas department store.

idahocafe.tumblr.com
Caroline Street, Cork

Lettercollum Kitchen Project, Clonakilty, Cork

Family run cafe and deli, producing most of their vegetables in their walled garden nearby. Wonderful cakes, quiches, scones and an excellent vegetarian selection, a rare thing still in Ireland.

lettercollum.ie
22, Connolly Street, Clonakilty, Co. Cork

Sage, Midleton, Co. Cork

Young chef Kevin Aherne has infused his strong personality and sense of place into this great restaurant and cafe. His "12 Mile" menu is the one that is making most noise right now, with all the produce sourced within 12 miles of Midleton from Cork's bountiful land, rivers and sea.

sagerestaurant.ie
The Courtyard, Main Street, Midleton, Co. Cork

Campagne, Kilkenny, Co. Kilkenny

An Irish chef does classic French cuisine in the heart of Ireland. Accomplished cooking and superb flavours here from Campagne's starry chef, Garret Byrne.

campagne.ie

5, The Arches, Gas House Lane, Kilkenny

Larder, Waterford, Co. Waterford

A tiny coffee shop and Irish artisan deli on the Quay in Waterford. Good soups, salads, scones, cakes, sourdough bread and, of course, fresh Waterford Blaas.

facebook.com/pages/Larder

111a, the Quay, Waterford

The Tannery, Dungarvan, Co. Waterford

One of the most loved restaurants in Ireland owned by one of the country's best loved chefs, Paul Flynn. A regular on Irish TV, that does not keep him from his kitchens or his cookery school just across the road. A really lovely, light space with the iron beams and skylights of the old tannery still intact, and an equally lovely welcome from Paul's wife, Máire, as you arrive.

tannery.ie

10 Quay Street, Dungarvan, Co. Waterford

Ardkeen Quality Food Store, Waterford

Founded by Pamela and Colin Jephson in 1967 "with petrol pumps out the front", Ardkeen is now Ireland's finest independent food retailer, showcasing the very best of Irish artisan produce.

ardkeen.com

Dunmore Road, Co. Waterford

The Cliff House, Ardmore, Co. Waterford

Perched high on a cliff overlooking the blue, blue bay and a stone's throw from *très chic* Ardmore village, this small 5 star hotel houses a terrific fine dining restaurant and a relaxed bar and grill, with broad terraces overlooking the sea. At once invigorating and completely luxurious.

thecliffhousehotel.com

Middle Road, Ardmore, Co. Cork

Rohu's Country Market, Innishannon, Co. Cork

Housed in a former courthouse that became a garage, Thomas and Michelle's country market is a lovely Irish shopping experience. Full of local artisan produce from Cork and beyond, there's great coffee, sofas and a woodburning stove if you'd like to linger a while after stocking up.

facebook.com/pages/Rohus-Country-Market

Main Road, Innishannon, Cork

Farmgate Cafes, Midleton and The English Market, Co. Cork

"Simple market food with a traditional and modern Irish Cork accent", says the blurb, but the cooking at these two iconic Irish addresses is something else. Probably the best spot for trying true Irish classic dishes, made the way they should be, using the very best produce. Unmissable.

farmgate.ie/corkhome.htm

Farmgate Cafe, The English Market, Princes St, Cork
Broderick St, Coolbawn, Midleton, Co. Cork

The English Market, Cork City, Co. Cork

Alongside St Georges Market in Belfast, and housed in an equally splendid building, The English market is one of Ireland's oldest and most authentic popular food markets (trading since 1788) and a Irish foodie experience not to be missed.

englishmarket.ie

Grand Parade, Cork

The Porcelain Room, Ballydehob, West Cork

Mediterranean cafe by day, Asian-Fusion restaurant by night, Joanne has brought back a wealth of culinary ideas and flavours from her travels to eclectic, buzzy Ballydehob.

porcelainroom.wordpress.com

Staball Hill, Ballydehob, + 353 87 926 3255

Ma Murphy's Bantry, West Cork

One of the most famous and popular pubs in West Cork. A genuine, untampered-with Irish bar, with a little grocery in the front and a long, dark bar through the back.

facebook.com/MaMurphysBar

7 New Street, Bantry

Hackett's Bar, Schull, West Cork

A beautiful little traditional bar, serving really good, fresh pub grub. Unbeatable for a simple bowl of soup with soda bread and a pint of Guinness for lunch at one of the shared tables or in the snug little rooms behind the bar. Great music too.

facebook.com/hacketts.bar

Main Street, Schull, West Cork

Ballymaloe House and Cookery School, Co. Cork

An Irish institution and the beating heart of Ireland's food renaissance. At once a restaurant, country house hotel, events hub and world-class cookery school. A trip (pilgrimage ?) to Ballymaloe is a must for anyone interested in Ireland's food heritage and future.

Shanagarry, Co. Cork

Ballymaloe.ie

The West: Bantry to Sligo

Wild Honey Inn, Lisdoonvarna

A tall and handsome building with rooms, a great bar and a romantic dining room adjacent, it's a spot much loved by visitors to the Burren. The Wild Honey Inn serves a terrific gastropub-ish menu from chef Aidan McGrath. Perfect for a celebratory meal.

wildhoneyinn.com

Kincora Rd, Lisdoonvarna, Co. Clare

Gregans Castle Hotel, Ballyvaughan

One of the most beautiful settings in Ireland for this super luxurious small hotel. And David Hurley's fine dining menu does justice to the incredible views over the Burren from the plush dining room. Afternoon teas are served on the lawn or in front of an open turf fire.

gregans.ie

Corkscrew Hill, Ballyvaughan, Co. Clare

Kai, Galway

Jess Murphy's energy and love of taste (and butter!) shine through in her super inventive, fresh cooking. One of Ireland's favourite restaurants, Kai is constantly packed.

kaicaferestaurant.com

20 Sea Road, Galway

Loam, Galway

Enda McAvoy won a Michelin star at Aniar in Galway before leaving to start Loam. His trailblazing cooking style owes much to the Nordic chefs, but his stamp on the finest wild Irish produce is unique.

loamgalway.com

Loam, Geata na Cathrach, Fairgreen, Galway

Ard Bia, Galway

In an old stone building, right by the river Corrib, Aoibheann McNamara and her team serve wonderful Irish food with a Mediterranean twist. Cakes and breakfasts are second to none in Ireland.

ardbia.com

Spanish Arch, Long Walk, Galway

Hargadon's pub, Sligo

One of the most beautiful pub interiors in Ireland, with lots of cosy, wood clad, hideaway snugs, and a super jolly, efficient staff serving very decent pub grub. Food is locally sourced and organic where possible.

hargadons.com

5 O'Connell St, Sligo

McCambridge's, Galway

This family owned deli and fine foods shop has a new, beautifully designed, modern, airy restaurant on the first floor. A Galway institution not to be missed.

mccambridges.com

38-39 Shop St, Galway, Co. Galway

Sheridans Wine bar, Galway

Another outpost of Sheridans' superlative cheese and fine food shops, this one has a handy wine bar upstairs with high tables and views over St Nicholas church and the lively weekend market on the square.

sheridanscheesemongers.com

14 Church Yard Street, Galway

Mulcahy's, Kenmare

Bruce Mulcahy has a wonderful understanding and mastery of Irish ingredients. This is smashing food, in a great restaurant, with super service. Not always easy to find in these very touristic corners of Ireland.

36 Henry Street, Kenmare, Co. Kerry

+ 353 64 6642383

+ 353 87 2364449

Country Choice, Nenagh

Peter Ward was, along with Myrtle and Darina Allen from Ballymaloe, one of Ireland's first food revolutionaries. He continues to champion local and organic produce in his bustling deli, food shop and cafe in the pretty country town of Nenagh.

countrychoice.ie

25 Kenyon Street, Nenagh, Co. Tipperary

Inis Meáin, Aran Islands

One of the most exclusive tables in Ireland, requiring quite a bit of planning to book, since the restaurant is on an island and only accessible by ferry. The austere luxury of the extraordinary architecture and superb cuisine created by owners Marie-Thérèse and Ruairí de Blacam will blow you away.

inismeain.com

Inis Meáin Restaurant & Suites, Inis Meáin, Aran Islands, Co. Galway

An Fear Gorta / The Tea & Garden Rooms, Ballyvaughan

Jane O Donoghue's gorgeous cakes, scones and tarts are worth skipping lunch for, and the gardens of her tea rooms a perfect place to rest a while after walking the Burren.

tearoomsballyvaughan.com

The Tea & Garden Rooms, Coast Road, Ballyvaughan, County Clare

The Roadside Tavern, Lisdoonvarna

One of the oldest pubs in the Burren district, the Roadside manages that seemingly impossible task of being pretty inside, serving really good food and programming fantastic Irish music — there's an outdoor stage when the weather allows. The Roadside belongs to the Curtin family, also of the Burren Smokehouse, so make sure you try the salmon.

roadsidetavern.ie

The Roadside Tavern Lisdoonvarna, Co. Clare

Places to stay

The Merchant Hotel, Belfast

5 star luxury in a spectacular building with Belfast's best cocktail bar.

themerchanthotel.com

16 Skipper Street, Belfast, County Antrim BT1 2DZ

Ballyvolane House, Co. Cork

Understated luxury and incomparable fun and hospitality in this beautiful family run country house.

ballyvolanehouse.ie

Castlelyons, Fermoy, Co. Cork

Cashel House Hotel, Connemara

Traditional and romantic country house hotel tucked away in a corner of Connemara.

cashelhouse.ie

Cashel, Connemara, Co. Galway

Perryville House Hotel, Kinsale

An imposing and elegant townhouse with superb bedrooms and gorgeous views over Kinsale harbour.

perryvillehouse.com

Kinsale, Co. Cork

Cliff house hotel, Ardmore, Co. Waterford

A super luxury hotel with a Michelin starred restaurant and sleek modern architecture, perched high on a cliff over the sea.

thecliffhousehotel.com

Merrion Hotel, Dublin

Discreet and luxurious, with a breathtaking art collection, lovely sitting rooms with turf lit fires and one of the country's best gourmet restaurants.

Merrion Street Upper, Dublin 2

merrionhotel.com

No 31, Dublin

A very smart, quirky, super quiet boutique guest house with a fabulous breakfast and gorgeous rooms.

number31.ie

31 Leeson Cl, Dublin 2

Gregans Castle Hotel, The Burren, Co. Clare

Superb setting, quiet and secluded luxury in one of Ireland's most striking landscapes.

gregans.ie

Corkscrew Hill, Ballyvaughan, Co. Clare

Mount Juliet, Thomastown, Co. Kilkenny

A very grand Country House set on a sweeping estate with the golf course and riding school.

mountjuliet.ie

Moy House, Lahinch

Beautiful décor in the old bedrooms, a private beach and superb sea views.

moyhouse.com

An Leacht, Lahinch, Co. Clare

Tankardstown House, Co. Meath
Perfect sense of hospitality in this lovely country house retreat, with gourmet food cooked from garden produce.
tankardstown.ie
Tankardstown, Co. Meath

Lough Bishop House, Westmeath
Warm and comfy B&B on this working farm that breeds rare native Irish Moiled cattle.
Derrynagarra, Collinstown, Co. Westmeath, Irlande
loughbishophouse.com

Ballynahinch Castle, Connemara
The ultimate in Irish luxury accommodation and hospitality, with serious fly fishing in the river running at the foot of the castle.
ballynahinch-castle.com
Recess, Connemara, Co. Galway

Cnoc Suain, Connemara
Beautiful thatched cottage accommodation and Irish music and culture in the wild heart of Connemara.
cnocsuain.com

Tannery Rooms, Dungarvan
Beautifully decorated and appointed rooms, perfect after an evening in Paul Flynn's restaurant accross the road.
tannery.ie
10 Quay St, Dungarvan, Co. Waterford

Delphi Lodge, Connemara
A perfect Irish country house, in an idyllic setting in the heart of the Connemara mountains and lakes.
delphilodge.ie
Delphi Valley, Connemara, Co. Galway

Plus

Hidden Ireland
The ultimate collection of luxury, stately family homes and country houses offering guest accommodation. A wonderful way to become immersed in Ireland's history.
hiddenireland.com

The Blue Book
A collection of unique country houses, historic hotels, manor houses, castles and restaurants in Ireland.
irelands-blue-book.ie

UTT
At the risk of sending you off elsewhere in the UK and Europe as you browse UTT's superbly located and decorated properties for holiday rent, have a look at their beautiful, wild yet cosy Donegal cottages.
underthethatch.co.uk

Guides and websites

McKennas Guides
Sally and John McKenna are Ireland's most renowned and accomplished food critics, authors and campaigners. Their guides and apps are terrific, notably a new guide to where to stay on the Wild Atlantic Way.
guides.ie

Georgina Campbell
The most comprehensive Irish guide to restaurants, pubs, activities and accommodation by leading writer and critic Georgina Campbell.
ireland-guide.com

Lovin' Dublin
Niall Harbison does not mince his words. This site is the most straight-talking and street you will find in Ireland right now. As well as restaurant reviews, there's lots of information on Dublin events, newsy items, and even recipes if you prefer to stay in and cook.
lovindublin.com

Lovin' Belfast
The city of Belfast's blog gives you everything you need to know about Belfast right now. From Belfast by bike, to what to do on a rainy day, it's all here.
visit-belfast.com/lovin-belfast

Online stores for Irish Products

Indie Fudie
An independant company sourcing locally handmade Irish products. Deliveries throughout UK, Ireland and Europe.
indiefude.com

BiaBeag
A marvellous resource for Irish artisan produce, collated by Keith Bohanna. Irish products available via mail order are all listed here.
biabeagonline.com

Food Tours
A website listing food tours in the Republic of Ireland.
fabfoodtrails.ie

Food and bar tours in Belfast and surroundings
belfastfoodtour.com
04610468684

Farmers' markets
Two sources of up to date information about Ireland's ever-growing farmers' markets.
irishfarmersmarkets.ie
bordbia.ie

Cookery schools
The Irish Tourist Board's website is a fantastic resource for all things food, including a good round-up of cookery courses and schools.
http://www.discoverireland.ie/Things-To-Do/Food-in-Ireland

Tourism and travel
discoverireland.ie
nationalairlines.ie
aerlingus.com
irishpassengerferries.com
irishferries.com

Irish Food Board
Bordbia.ie

RECIPES INDEX

SOME FURTHER READING

Beyond James Joyce, here are my favourite books from my 'Home' reading list.
Some are about food and cookery, others give (often very funny) insight into Ireland's society, past and present.

Darina ALLEN   *Irish Traditional Cooking* (Kyle Books)

Colman ANDREWS   *The Country Cooking of Ireland* (Chronicle)

Alison ARMSTRONG   *The Joyce of Cooking* (Station Hill Press).

Georgina CAMPBELL   *Ireland for Food Lovers* (GC Guides)

Clare CONNERY   *Irish Food and Folklore* (Bounty Books)

Richard CORRIGAN   *The Clatter of Forks and Spoons* (4th Estate)

Tamasin DAY LEWIS   *West of Ireland Summers* (Orion)

Theodora FITZGIBBON   *A Taste of Ireland* (Pan Books)

Mr and Mrs SC HALL   *Hall's Ireland* (Sphere)

Florence IRWIN   *The Cookin' Woman* (The Blackstaff Press)

Margaret JOHNSON   *Cooking with Irish Spirits* (Wolfhound Press)

John B KEANE   *Strong Tea* (The Mercier Press)

Mollie KEANE   *Good Behaviour* (Virago)

Ben LANDER   *Irish Voices Irish Lives* (Brandon)

Maura LAVERTY   *Full and Plenty* (Anvil)

Biddy WHITE LENNON   *Festive Cooking* (O'Brien Best of Irish)

Éamonn MACTHOMÁIS   *Gur Cakes and Coal* (O'Brien Press)

Pete McCARTHY   *McCarthy's Bar* (Sceptre)

John McGUFFIN   *In Praise of Poteen* (Appletree)

John and Sally McKENNA   *Extreme Greens* (Estragon Press)

Maurice O SULLIVAN   *Twenty Years a Growing* (Oxford Press)

Prannie RHATIGAN   *Irish Seaweed Kitchen* (Booklink)

David THOMSON   *Woodbrook* (Vintage)

Regina SEXTON   *A little history of Irish Food* (Kyle Books)

SOMERVILLE AND ROSS   *The Irish RM* (Faber and Faber)

BIA COOK BOOK

Morning, Lunchtime, Afternoon, Evening, After Dinner & Pantry

jenateone an Irish food story

A CELEBRATION OF
THE WORLD-RENOWNED
COOKERY SCHOOL WITH
OVER 100 NEW RECIPES

Books in the guest's sitting room, Ballyvolane, Co. Cork

ACKNOWLEDGEMENTS

Firstly to all the great Irish food writers whose work has inspired and guided me, Darina Allen, Biddy White Lennon, Sally and John McKenna, Georgina Campbell, Florence Irwin and Theodora FitzGibbon.

I'm very grateful to the friends and fellow food-world dwellers I have pestered so much over the past few years about all manner of things edible and Irish. Notably Roz and Bill Crowley, Seamus Hogan, Sophie Flynn-Rogers, Joe Macnamee, Catriona Redmund, Ella McSweeney, Peter Alexander, Joris Minne, Donal Doherty, Seamus Sheridan, Enda McEvoy, Conor Cockram, Tim Magee, Marie Claire Digby and Orna Mulcahy.

Huge thanks for your help, generosity and hospitality during my travels & shooting of the book to Frank and Caroline Hederman, Stevie Toman, Alain Kerloc'h, Hannah Massey, OX, Michael Wade and Pascal Marinot at Delphi Lodge, Cashel House Hotel, Connemara, the Calvey family, Achill Mountain Lamb, Tom Doorley, Nuala Hickey, Hickey's bakery, Clonmel Noreen and Martin Conroy, Woodside Farm, Kevin Aherne, Sage, Peter Hannan, Hannan Meats, Simon and Freddie Haden, Gregans Castle Hotel, Will Brown, Old Schoolhouse Inn, the Cliff House Hotel, Dublin, Graham Neville, Restaurant Forty One, Maire and Paul Flynn, The Tannery, Aoibheann MacNamara, Ard Bia, Cliodhna Prendergast and Patrick O'Flaherty, Ballynahinch Castle, Patricia Conroy, Tankardstown House, Mario Sierra, Mourne Textiles, Host PR, Fionntan Gogarty, Wildwood Vinegars, Jonathan McDowell, Indie Fudie, Donal Doherty, Harry's Bridgend, Pat Whelan, Whelan's Butchers, Phillip Moss, Filligans Jams, Alison and Will Abernethy, Abernethy butter.

We've had great support for "Home" from Bord Bia, Tourism Ireland, Irish Ferries, Aer Lingus and The National Trust, Northern Ireland. Special thanks to Noreen Lanigan, Anne Zemmour, Clair Balmer, Esther Dobbin and Martine McKenna.

Thank you for letting us invade and helping us to make the book beautiful! The Cole family at Broughgammon Farm, Donald Alexander at The Burn, Wilbert Robinson at Standing Stone Farm, Brian and Vibse Dunleath at Ballywalter Estate, Jenny and Justin Green at Ballyvolane House, Ina Daly at Daly's pub, Ballydehob, the McHughs at Nancy's, Ardara, Paula Scally, Green Gate, Ardara, Dearbhaill Standún and Charlie Troy, Cnoc Suain, Connemara.

I'm very honoured to have such wonderful contributors in the book, thanks to: Darina Allen, Joe MacNamee, Pat Whelan, Seamus Hogan, Mark Diacono, Seamus Sheridan, Caroline Hederman, Robbie Krawczyk, Jess Murphy, Enda McEvoy, Carmel Somers, David Hurley, Derek Creagh, Graham Neville, Stevie Toman, my Auntie Beattie, Richard Corrigan, Peter Ward, Dermot Staunton and Auntie Olga.

To my fantastic team in Hachette, Paris: Isabelle Magnac, Catherine Saunier-Talec, Johanna Rodrigues-Faitot, Lisa Grall, Antoine Béon, Celine Le Lamer in Paris, Ben Wright in London and Siobhán Tierney and Jim Binchy in Dublin. Merci l'équipe!

Many thanks to Anna Gyseman for all her help with the book's design, Audrey Stafford for the copy editing and proof reading and of course to the super-talented photographer, Deirdre "mountain goat" Rooney.

And most of all, a thank you to my daughter Victoire who fills me with pride every day, and to whom I dedicate Home, with love.

Bar in Galway

Rain coming in over the Iveragh peninsula, Co. Kerry.